D1473097

THE
EISENHOWER
LEGACY

THE EISENHOWER LEGACY

DISCUSSIONS OF PRESIDENTIAL LEADERSHIP

EDITED BY
SHIRLEY ANNE WARSHAW

Foreword by Gerald R. Ford

Bartleby Press
Silver Spring, Maryland

Printed in the United States of America

Published and Distributed by:

Bartleby Press
11141 Georgia Avenue
Silver Spring, Maryland 20902

Library of Congress Cataloging-in-Publication Data

The Eisenhower legacy: discussions of presidential leadership / edited
    by Shirley Anne Warshaw : foreword by Gerald R. Ford.
      p.   cm.
    Includes index.
    ISBN 0-910155-21-6 (hardcover) : $16.95
    1. Eisenhower, Dwight D. (Dwight David), 1890-1969—Congresses.
    2. United States—Politics and government—1953-1961—Congresses.
    3. Political leadership—United States—History—20th century—
Congresses.   I. Warshaw, Shirley Anne, 1950-
E836.E35   1992
973.921'092—dc20   92-736

Contents

Foreword

The year 1990 marked the nation's tribute to the 100th birthday of one of our greatest presidents: Dwight David Eisenhower. I was privileged to participate in the celebration of the centennial of Eisenhower's birth held by Gettysburg College throughout the week of October 14th, 1990.

My relationship with President Eisenhower began in that fateful year of 1952. I had been in Congress for two terms by that time and realized the necessity of strong presidential leadership. In February 1952, eighteen of us in the Congress sent a message to Dwight D. Eisenhower asking him to run for President as a Republican. The leading Republican candidate at the time was Senator Robert Taft of Ohio, but his foreign policy views were too isolationist for my taste. Furthermore, I was convinced that Ike could win in November and after nearly twenty years of Democratic presidents the country needed a change. I was delighted, of course, when Ike won the nomination and, later, the election.

The presidency of Dwight David Eisenhower is marked by outstanding accomplishments in both domestic and foreign policy, and also in the organizational structure that he brought to policy making. President Eisenhower's leadership has been chronicled in numerous scholarly books, but the centennial celebration at Gettysburg College provided us an unparalleled opportunity to understand more fully President Eisenhower's leadership style.

Never in the nearly thirty years since President Eisenhower left office has there been an examination of this caliber to examine the successes and failures of the two terms of the Eisenhower presidency. Gettysburg College assembled the largest gathering of Eisenhower staff and Cabinet since the administration left office, providing a wealth of discussion and material on the "inside" workings of the White House.

The Eisenhower presidency was committed to a strong international role for the U.S. and to firm management of the burgeoning growth of the federal budget. These, of course, were difficult tasks but ones that were skillfully if not brilliantly handled by the political leadership of Dwight David Eisenhower.

Eisenhower's many contributions to the institution of the presidency included an expanded role for the National Security Council and the creation of a Special Assistant for National Security Affairs to advise the President on national affairs.

Eisenhower's National Security Council system was organized to ensure for the benefit of the President the systematic presentation of independent and alternative viewpoints in this critical area. It was because of Eisenhower's strong model that my national security advisory system was able to act swiftly in the Mayaquez incident. Every subsequent administration has used the national security advisory system put in place by President Eisenhower in differing degrees of influence, procedures and control.

There is, of course, a more personal side to the Eisenhower legacy and that is the relationship of the public to President Eisenhower. People loved him. As you know, I sought to be extremely open with the press, a commitment I learned from watching Ike. Eisenhower was the first President to let reporters tape record news conferences and even some private conversations with reporters. From about 1955 on, Eisenhower could be seen regularly on the evening news with Douglas Edwards.

We owe Dwight Eisenhower a great deal, but perhaps one of the most enduring legacies of the Eisenhower years is one all too many people know little about, and that is the area of civil rights. Dwight Eisenhower was the first modern President to actively take up the mantle for civil rights, and we all owe him a great debt of gratitude. President Eisenhower moved to end discrimination in federal employment and in employment by federal contractors; to end segregation in Washington, D.C.—the nation's capital; to desegregate the armed forces; and named unprecedented numbers of blacks to positions in the executive branch, including Frederic Morrow, who became a senior member of the White House staff. Under President Eisenhower's leadership, two major civil rights bills were passed and the federal judiciary was carefully structured to include appointees who supported a strong federal role in civil rights.

Any discussion of the domestic agenda would not be complete

without mentioning President Eisenhower's magnificent contribution to the nation's role in space. Under the guidance of the President, Congress created the National Aeronautics and Space Administration on July 29, 1958. The creation of NASA indicated in yet another way the strong leadership of President Eisenhower. After the launching of Sputnik by the Russians, there was a national clamor to increase our military space program to ensure that we did not fall behind the Russians in our capabilities to launch intercontinental ballistic missiles. However, President Eisenhower saw the importance of a national space program that was directed not only at military ends but also to the scientific advantages of space exploration. He pursued a national space agency not designed exclusively for military purposes, as many wanted, but for overall scientific investigation. Eisenhower stressed that the fundamental challenge posed by Sputnik was educational rather than military. Due to President Eisenhower's extraordinary leadership, Congress moved to create a national space agency whose primary goal was scientific. Space would not be militarized under the Eisenhower Administration.

Finally, let me note that the Eisenhower Administration will stand out for untold generations to come for its decision to assume responsibility for the reconstruction of Europe and Asia after World War II. In spite of strong political pressure to turn inward, Eisenhower moved swiftly and decisively, as he had so many times in battle, to ensure the strength of the European and the Japanese economies. President Eisenhower forged a new economic and political alliance with both Europe and Japan which endures today.

It is this legacy that we celebrated at Gettysburg. The discussions in this book provide numerous insights into the Eisenhower administration, most from a personal perspective. I was proud to be part of this program and know that these discussions will provide the world with a unique look into President Eisenhower's strong character, leadership style, and the many accomplishments of his administration.

—Gerald R. Ford

Introduction

A s the nation moves nearer to the twenty-first century, we have begun to closely examine the legacy of the twentieth century. Certainly one of the most influential men of this century was Dwight David Eisenhower, who led the free world to victory in World War II, presided over the rebuilding of Europe as the Supreme Allied Commander, and guided the United States through the Cold War as President.

Throughout 1990, the centennial year of President Eisenhower's birth, the nation paid homage to one of its true heroes. The Congress of the United States held a joint session honoring President Eisenhower, and President Bush held a ceremony at the White House for Eisenhower friends and family.

Among the many tributes to President Eisenhower was an international symposium held at Gettysburg College in Gettysburg, Pennsylvania. Gettysburg had been the home of President and Mrs. Eisenhower for twenty years after World War II. President Eisenhower loved the Gettysburg area and throughout his presidency spent weekends and vacations at his farm.

President Eisenhower's relationship with the Gettysburg community began in 1915 when, as a senior cadet at West Point, he travelled to Gettysburg to study the battlefield. Three years later he returned to Gettysburg as the commander of Camp Colt, a training center for the Tank Corps, being readied for overseas assignments during World War I, and which was housed adjacent to the battlefield.

During the summer of 1918, Captain and Mrs. Eisenhower stayed at what was then the Alpha Tau Omega fraternity house on the Gettysburg College campus. When the students returned to campus in the fall, the Eisenhowers moved to another residence close to the campus.

In November of 1918, Captain Eisenhower left Camp Colt for a new appointment at Fort Dix, New Jersey. His military career continued until the late 1940's, when he retired as a five-star general. In June of 1948, Columbia University convinced Eisenhower to take its helm. Throughout his term at Columbia University, Eisenhower remained active in the national arena, serving in various roles for President Truman. In December 1948, he became a military consultant to James Forrestal, Secretary of Defense, and in the spring of 1949, he became an informal chairman of the Joints Chiefs of Staff. His tenure at Columbia University was brief, however, for in 1950, he took a leave of absence at the request of President Truman to accept the appointment as Supreme Allied Commander of the newly established North American Treaty Organization (NATO).

Due to his assignments across the country and the world, President and Mrs. Eisenhower did not return to Gettysburg for almost thirty years after his tenure at Camp Colt. In 1946 he accepted an honorary Doctor of Laws from Gettysburg College. His warm experiences with Gettysburg College and the Gettysburg community convinced Dwight and Mamie Eisenhower to seek a permanent home in the area. In 1950 they found a 190-acre farm complete with a barn and a house and quickly purchased it. Surrounded by the Gettysburg Battlefield, the farm was located just west of Seminary Ridge, the staging site of Pickett's Charge on July 3, 1863. "The buildings had seen better days," Eisenhower wrote in his memoirs. "So had the soil. It would take work and money to modernize it. But the view of the mountains to the west was good."

The Eisenhowers immediately began to restore the farmhouse on the property, with the hopes of moving right in. Of the thirty-seven houses they had lived in, this would be the only one they would call home. They discovered, however, the brick farmhouse surrounded an old log cabin, which was too deteriorated to save. As a result, they tore down the original house and built a new one. They managed to save one wall and a Dutch oven from the original farmhouse. The farm soon became the focus of the Eisenhower family. The Eisenhowers raised Angus cows on the meadows and brought their children and grandchildren together for numerous family visits. Grandson David Eisenhower was a frequent visitor and often spent his summer afternoons painting the fences around the farm.

The farm was not only a private retreat but also served in an official capacity. During his two terms as President, Eisenhower invited numerous world leaders to Gettysburg, including Jawaharlal Nehru, General Charles de Gaulle, Sir Winston Churchill, Field Marshall Viscount Bernard Montgomery, Chancellor Konrad Adenauer, and Premier Nikita Khruschev.

For a brief period in 1955, from November 14th through December 20th, Gettysburg served as the White House. President Eisenhower recuperated from his heart attack at his farm, and the White House staff used the U.S. Post Office as their headquarters. During that recuperation, President Eisenhower delivered the annual Christmas message to the nation from the Gettysburg College campus. Using the office of the college president in Glatfelter Hall, President Eisenhower spoke and then pressed a gold telegraph key to turn on the Christmas tree lights in Washington, D.C.

His official use of the Gettysburg College facilities included a major foreign policy statement in April 1959, at the college's Convocation. As he prepared for the Paris summit in May on disarmament, Eisenhower delivered a clear word of warning to Nikita Khruschev on the free-city status of East and West Berlin. "The course of appeasement is not only dishonorable, it is the most dangerous one we could pursue. The world paid a high price for the lesson of Munich, but it learned it well."

After his term of office ended in January of 1961, President Eisenhower retired to his farm and used the offices of Gettysburg College for meetings and to write his memoirs. The college gave the President and his staff the use of a building on campus, which is today known as Eisenhower House. During the next eight years, Eisenhower wrote three volumes: *The White House Years: Mandate for Change (1953-56)* (1963); *Waging Peace (1956-1961)* (1965); and *At East: Stories I Tell to Friends* (1967). He was also a member of the college's Board of Trustees from 1961 until his death in 1969 and was an active participant in college decisions.

As a result of this long relationship with President Eisenhower, Gettysburg College hosted the Eisenhower Symposium during the week of October 10-14, 1990. October 14th marked the 100th birthday of Dwight David Eisenhower. The Symposium brought together members of the Eisenhower cabinet and staff, members of the press, and scholars from around the world to assess the Eisenhower presidency. This was the largest gathering of Eisenhower staff in over thirty years.

The outcome of this gathering was an exciting and dynamic series of discussions on the Eisenhower presidency and, perhaps more importantly, on the President himself. For the first time, many members of the cabinet and staff openly discussed how President Eisenhower approached the economy, civil rights, the McCarthy hearings, the press, the Cold War, and numerous other topics.

One of the keystones of the Eisenhower presidency was the administration's ability to maintain a balanced budget three times. As a tribute for performing the "political miracle of making the economy popular," *Time* magazine named President Eisenhower their 1959 Man of the Year. Among the participants in the discussion about domestic policy were Raymond Saulnier, Chairman of the Council of Economic Advisers, and Maurice Stans, Director of the Bureau of the Budget. Each examined Eisenhower's views on economic planning and the balanced budget.

The issue of civil rights became one of the most controversial subjects of the Eisenhower years, particularly as a result of the 1954 *Brown v. Board of Education* decision by the Supreme Court. Although the Supreme Court mandated only that school districts approach desegretation with "all deliberate speed," President Eisenhower pursued an end to school desegregation.

In addition, President Eisenhower moved to end discrimination in federal employment and in employment by federal contractors, to desegregate the armed forces, and to appoint unprecedented numbers of blacks to senior positions in the executive branch, including the White House staff. It is important to note that before the *Brown* decision had been rendered by the Supreme Court, President Eisenhower ordered the end to segregation in the city of Washington, D.C. which is under the jurisdiction of the federal government.

The Eisenhower administration successfully moved two civil rights bills through Congress, the Civil Rights Bill of 1957 and the Civil Rights Bill of 1960. These bills, the first civil rights bills since Reconstruction, were primarily aimed at voting rights. Eisenhower's enforcement of both the voting rights legislation and the *Brown* decision included the creation of the Civil Rights Section in the Department of Justice and the hiring of nearly 600 federal marshalls to enforce school integration. The panelists discussing civil rights in the Eisenhower years included the chief White House strategist for civil rights, Rocco Siliano; the Attorney General and architect of the Civil Rights bills, Herbert Brownell; and the Secretary of Health, Education and Welfare, Arthur Flemming.

One of the most difficult periods of his presidency involved the tenacious activities of Senator Joseph McCarthy (R-Wisconsin). In trying to preserve relations with the Republican leadership in the Senate, Eisenhower had refused to publicly attack Senator McCarthy because of his Republican ties. The Republicans controlled the Senate by only one vote, and Eisenhower was leery of angering any Republican for fear of jeopardizing administration-sponsored legislation. However, McCarthy's refusal to support the confirmation of a Presidential nominee in the Senate and his continued attack on the U.S. army for harboring Communists led Eisenhower to publicly repudiate McCarthy. The McCarthy-Eisenhower relationship was discussed by a variety of speakers, including members of the press, the administration, and academia.

Another topic that dominated the presidency of Dwight Eisenhower was the burgeoning atomic age and how to manage it. Eisenhower was a strong proponent of nuclear weapons as a way to minimize the costs of deterrence. The expansionist drive of the Soviet government during the 1940's and 1950's had forced a military response by the Eisenhower government. Eisenhower retaliated against Soviet expansionism with a strong nuclear arsenal designed for both the NATO alliance and the United States. Yet, by reducing the size of the standing army and relying on a nuclear strategy, Eisenhower was able to cut the costs of America's military defense system.

However, his reliance on the nuclear arsenal for military objectives did not preclude his efforts for arms reductions. Arms control was the focus of two international initiatives: Atoms for Peace and Open Skies. The complex design of

Eisenhower's nuclear strategy is revealed by several speakers at the Eisenhower Symposium, including his grandson and biographer, David Eisenhower. David Eisenhower noted in his discussion of foreign policy that President Eisenhower's mandate from the American people in both the 1952 and 1956 elections was foreign policy, and how to manage the Cold War. The discussions during the Symposium point to a President preoccupied with international affairs.

Another area of both international and domestic concern touched on during the Eisenhower Symposium was the U-2 affair in 1960. On the afternoon of May 1st, President Eisenhower was told by General Andrew Goodpaster, that a U-2 reconnaissance plane had been shot down over the Soviet Union and its pilot presumed dead. The downing of the U-2 could not have come at a worse time, for Eisenhower was preparing for a U.S.-Soviet summit in Paris. If word spread that the U.S. was carrying out secret military reconnaissance flights over the Soviet Union, the summit would be jeopardized. Confident that the plane had been destroyed, President Eisenhower issued a statement on May 5th announcing that "One of NASA's U-2 research airplanes, in use since 1956 in a continuing program to study meteorological conditions found at high altitude, has been missing since May 1, when its pilot reported he was having oxygen difficulties over the Lake Van, Turkey area."

However, Khrushchev soon released a photograph of the American plane and announced that its pilot, Francis Gary Powers, had been captured. As a result, President Eisenhower was forced to admit the existence of the reconnaissance flight and to confirm that he had personally authorized its mission.

The decisions to at first deny and later to acknowledge the flight were both criticized, seriously damaging the President's reputation at home and abroad and eventually led to a failed Paris summit. The fate of the U-2 reconnaissance plane is detailed at length throughout the sessions.

There is also the human side of President Eisenhower that was seen so often at the Symposium. Bradley Patterson, the Deputy Secretary of the Cabinet, related Eisenhower's insistence that a prayer be said before each Cabinet meeting. Attorney General Herbert Brownell recounted Eisenhower's despair at having to remove Sherman Adams from his job as Chief of Staff. Daniel Schorr discussed the brilliant way in which Eisenhower maneuvered the press over and over again.

In the following pages, new insights emerge on the leadership style of President Eisenhower. What surfaces is a picture of a President committed to moving the nation into a new era, one of economic prosperity and international cooperation. It is a picture of an activist President with a clear agenda. Each of the speakers brings a depth of knowledge to the stage, most from first-hand experience.

Never again will the nation gather together such an outstanding group on the Eisenhower Presidency. The Eisenhower Symposium provided a unique look at the eight years that proved pivotal in both domestic and international policy. The nation had eight years of peace and prosperity in an increasingly turbulent international arena. The Eisenhower Symposium at Gettysburg College was a celebration of the centennial of President Eisenhower's birth, but more importantly was a unique opportunity to reexamine his presidency. The Eisenhower Legacy is a truly remarkable one, and continues to touch the life of every American today.

—**Shirley Anne Warshaw**
Department of Political Science
Gettysburg College

CHAPTER ONE

An Informal Discussion with Eisenhower Cabinet and Staff

This chapter involves informal discussion with key members of the Eisenhower Cabinet and staff presided over by Daniel Schorr. Schorr covered President Eisenhower for CBS news as its White House correspondent, and as such knew each member of the panel quite well. He was able to bring about a truly remarkable discussion on key domestic, economic, and foreign policy issues.

Among the most interesting subjects to arise in this session was the degree of interchange that President Eisenhower had with his advisors on every major issue confronting the administration. There has been some suggestion for a number of years that President Eisenhower was not concerned about the details of policy making and often deferred the decision making to his assistants. This line of thinking, however, is completely discounted throughout the discussions in this session. According to the panelists, President Eisenhower was actively involved in the decision-making process and guided that process to meet his agenda needs.

For example, Elmer Staats and Raymond Saulnier, two of the President's key economic advisers, provide ample detail of President Eisenhower's involvement in economic policy making, particularly in his views on supply side economics. They note that President Eisenhower saw a balanced budget as essential to a healthy economy, and mandated that each of his cabinet officers reduce spending until the balanced budget had been accomplished.

Elmer Staats also provides a long discussion on the mechanisms that President Eisenhower put in place for foreign policy analysis through the National Security Council and the Opera-

tions Coordinating Board. He carefully points out that national
security dominated a major portion of the President's time.
Throughout his eight years in office, President Eisenhower
faced crises in Korea, Lebanon, Egypt, Viet Nam, Latin America, and Formosa. In addition, the Soviet Union had become the
world's largest military force, with a constantly increasing
nuclear arsenal. How the United States contained Soviet aggression and protected itself from nuclear war controlled a majority
of foreign policy decisions.

As Dr. Glenn Seaborg, who discovered plutonium and won
the Nobel Prize in 1952 for that discovery, noted during the
panel, President Eisenhower was extremely concerned about
the potentially devastating role of nuclear weapons and pursued
every avenue for arms control. An example of his commitment
to arms control is the little known Antarctic Peace Treaty, which
both the Soviet Union and the United States signed under pressure from President Eisenhower. The treaty, which still prevails
today, provided that all weapons would be banned from the
Antarctic.

The panel also explored the Eisenhower-McCarthy relationship, including President Eisenhower's deep dislike for Senator
Joseph McCarthy. Since early 1950, Senator Joseph McCarthy
had waged a crusade against communism. He was one of numerous members of Congress who had launched investigations of
communist activities throughout the nation, including in federal
agencies. However, since Senator McCarthy was a prominent
Republican in Congress, President Eisenhower had refused to
attack him for fear of alienating his own party. Eisenhower's
strategy was to ignore McCarthy, hoping that his silence on
McCarthy would speak for itself.

One of the most absorbing discussions on the Eisenhower-
McCarthy relationship was provided by Attorney General Herbert Brownell. General Brownell details how President Eisenhower became infuriated at Senator McCarthy's suggestion that
he (President Eisenhower) was a communist and that many generals in the United States Army were communists, including
General George Marshall. As Attorney General Brownell said, "I
saw him completely lose his temper" on hearing this, and say
'We've got to stop this'."

The panel also turned to President Eisenhower's handling of the U-2 affair. In late 1954, at the suggestion of the Director of Central Intelligence, Allen Dulles, Eisenhower authorized the use of reconnaissance planes over the Soviet Union. His decision to proceed with the reconnaissance planes was based on the availability of new technology. Lockheed had just developed a single jet engine plane capable of flying long distances at an altitude of over seventy thousand feet. In addition, Edwin H. Land, the inventor of the Polaroid-Land camera, had devised a new process that was capable of high-level precision photography. Eisenhower made the decision to pursue the reconnaissance flights, in spite of some chance the planes would be detected by the Soviets.

After nearly six years of successful reconnaissance flights, the United States lost a reconnaissance plane to Soviet fire in 1960. The Soviets shot down the plane and captured the pilot, Francis Gary Powers. Although his advisors recommended "plausible deniability", as Bradley Patterson recounts, President Eisenhower insisted that "everybody is going to say that I was out playing golf, and wasn't running my government and I'm not going to do that. I'm going to take responsibility." Daniel Schorr comments on that decision as a major mistake, adding, "There are things which Presidents should not take responsibility for." This became one of the great crises of the Eisenhower administration, and one which remains hotly debated among scholars. Did President Eisenhower make the right decision by acknowledging the reconnaissance flight or should he have pursued the tactic of "plausible deniability." Clearly there are many facets to this issue, some of which are looked at in this session.

In summary, this session provides wide-ranging discussions on numerous aspects of the Eisenhower Presidency by some of the key players in his administration.

PANEL

Moderator: **Daniel Schorr,** *National Public Radio*

Panelists:

Herbert Brownell	*Attorney General of the U.S., 1953-57*
Glenn Seaborg	*Member of Science Advisory Committee (PSAC), 1959-61, Chairman, U.S. Atomic Energy Commission, 1961-71*
Elmer Staats	*Executive Officer, Operations Coordinating Board (OCB), National Security Council 1953-58*
Raymond Saulnier	*Chairman, Council of Economic Advisers, 1956-60*
Bradley H. Patterson, Jr.	*Deputy Secretary to the Cabinet, the White House, 1954-61*

Daniel Schorr: I will not be long. This is the beginning of several days in which we will look at an extraordinary person who served America at an extraordinary time in our history. The program indicates that, as we go on in other days and other evenings, there will be ample opportunity for scholars to examine his contributions to history. I would like tonight to be a different sort of evening. I am the moderator—I make those decisions. Some people think that, for me, moderator is an oxymoron, but never mind.

First, let me tell you a little bit about my Eisenhower connection, but very briefly. In the more than seventy years that I have lived, one decade was what I call my Eisenhower decade. In 1950, I was serving as a correspondent for the *New York Times* in western Europe when General Eisenhower came back to Europe to become the Supreme Commander of NATO forces. As you will constantly have to be reminded, with most of you being too young to have lived through very much of this, I'm speaking of a period when Europe was beginning to arise from the ruins of World War II; unsure of itself, unsure of where it was going and rather unsure, in spite of the need for armed forces, whether they really wanted armed forces. One of the functions of General Eisenhower was to inspire these countries, inspire their civilian leaders to understand the need for unity and the need for NATO, which he did by just being himself.

One of those little stories I remember best as he roamed around these countries making speeches, showing the flag, showing fourteen flags, was when I covered him on his first inspection tour. I remember one occasion on an inspection trip to Belgium when he was shown the place where stores were being kept for the Belgium army. He saw two piles of blankets and said, "What are these two piles of blankets which look different?" And the Belgium general said, "Well, these are for the officers and these are for the enlisted men." And Eisenhower said, "Do the officers get colder or what?" That was the kind of thing he would say. Then he went back and became President of Columbia University, eventually agreed to run for office and, as it happened in 1953, about the time his first administration was starting, I went to work for CBS in Washington. I had another several years of covering President Eisenhower, not only in Washington but on trips to South America, trips to India and finally ending up in Paris in May, 1960, at the summit that wasn't. That is to say, the summit conference of the Four Powers which was broken up by Nikita Khrushchev storming out, angry not only because the United States had flown a U-2 spy plane over the Soviet Union but perhaps, more specifically, because President Eisenhower had taken responsibility for that spy plane. Khrushchev felt that made it very difficult for him to deal with President Eisenhower. Those were my ten years, filled with White House press conferences and stories about press conferences. I recall, for example, how hard we tried as we approached 1956, to find out whether he was going to run again for President. At a press conference he was asked what he thought of the proposal of the Republican National Committee to have a shorter campaign and a later convention in 1956. He said, "Well, if I were the candidate, I think that would be a good idea." People popped up, including myself, and said, "Mr. President, that sounds as though you're going to be the candidate." President Eisenhower said, "Oh, rubbish." That was the kind of person he was.

You are going to hear now from five persons who worked in the White House in very different capacities. I don't know how it came to be but by getting these five, we really see President Eisenhower from many points of view. I would like tonight to be an evening of unashamed nostalgia. You'll get the heavy stuff about his contributions later on between now and next Saturday. For now, here are some people who at one electrifying moment in history all found themselves working in one way or another for the same man. I've not seen many of them for many years. Some of them have not seen each other for many years. After Eisenhower life went on in many different ways, different preoccupations and different missions to be accomplished; but now, we want to roll back the calendar and turn back the clock to that time. I have very long biographies on all of them which I forgot to share with you but I'll only tell you now the functions served during the Eisenhower administration. All of them have gone on to do many other things.

Herbert Brownell, who, of course, was the Attorney General of the United States from 1953-1957.

Glenn Seaborg, who, in the Eisenhower time, was a member of PSAC, the President's Science Advisory Committee, the committee which he has said was very important to the President because he believed very strongly in the importance of science and technology. Dr. Seaborg later went on to become Chairman of the United States Atomic Energy Commission, but that was after the Eisenhower administration.

Elmer Staats who worked at first until about 1958 in the National Security Council and then, starting in 1958, became Deputy Director of the Bureau of the Budget. The bureau which is now headed by Richard Darman who has become a famous person on television and elsewhere.

Then, Raymond Saulnier, who was Chairman of the Council of Economic Advisors.

And Bradley Patterson, who was Deputy Secretary to the Cabinet from 1954 until 1961.

We have not had a lot of consultations here, I don't think a lot of consultations are necessary. I'm asking you to start this evening by thinking back to one anecdote, one episode, one incident of your dealing with President Eisenhower; how he dealt with you, what it was about, and hoping that in the course of doing that, we can help him become alive for this audience here. Let me start, because he was the Deputy Secretary of the Cabinet, with Mr. Patterson, who has a particular story to tell.

Bradley Patterson: Dan, my memory is particularly vivid about the most interesting Cabinet meeting in the Eisenhower administration. You remember, of course, that Eisenhower was the first President since Jefferson to use the Cabinet in a systematic fashion. He was also the first President in history to have the indispensable small staff unit, namely the Cabinet Secretariat, to help him do this. The first Cabinet Secretary was Max Rabb, and later, in 1958, Bob Gray; and I was the deputy to both of them. He insisted that every important domestic issue in the Eisenhower administration come to the Cabinet just as he brought the major national security issues to the National Security Council. Some of the meetings had some trivia, obviously, and some of them had items of medium interest but one meeting I remember in 1959, had a major question before the Cabinet and the Cabinet split wide open on it. This was the issue of aid to education. In 1959, the schools, you will remember, were crammed with baby boomers. The Democrats had put forward a very expensive proposal for aid to education, and Arthur Flemming, who was then Secretary of Health, Education and Welfare, put forward a modest proposal and he brought it to Eisenhower's office on a Thursday night. Ike was divided in his own mind. Flemming and Persons (Persons was Chief of Staff at the time) debated it in the Oval Office and finally Eisenhower said, "Arthur, bring it to Cabinet tomorrow morning." This is one example, and there were several, where Eisenhower set the Cabinet agenda himself with the command: "Get that paper on the agenda. Get Flemming to present it." So, at the Cabinet meeting of January 16, 1959, Flemming laid this out in his own ineffable way, tremendous energy, tremendous articulation, but Eisenhower introduced him by saying he had difficulty and problems with a proposal like this, it took away from the authority of the states and he believed deeply in our federal system and not undercutting the authority of the states. Then he said, "All right, Arthur, now I've put this noose around your neck, go ahead and make your presentation." That didn't stop Dr. Flemming for a minute. The Cabinet was deeply divided, Summerfield, the

Taftites, the folks who were on the conservative side. Benson jumped all over it because Eisenhower had given them the hint that he had some doubts about it. Then Secretary of Labor Mitchell spoke up and said, "I think education is a national resource." Then Mr. Nixon spoke up (remember this is 1959 and he was then the heir apparent) and he said, "Really, I believe I agree with Jim Mitchell." He said, "I think we ourselves need to do something." It was typical of the Eisenhower Cabinet, between the conservatives and the liberals, to have that kind of a candid airing back and forth and, in the end, Eisenhower, who at the beginning had been really apprehensive and doubtful, was turned around by the very forcefulness of Flemming's presentation and by the comments of the more liberal members of the Cabinet. He turned to Flemming and said, "All right, we'll do it; meet the leadership tomorrow," and then he turned to all of them and said, "Well, we've had a good growl." That's what the Cabinet meetings were for those seven years, they were good growls; but they came out, as I say, with all the major issues of the domestic policy in the Eisenhower administration. Nobody felt left out. Nobody felt ignored. Everybody had his say. Everybody could see the President making up his mind in front of them, expressing himself in strong language and see the results. They had a kind of teamwork which was illustrated by this little story.

Daniel Schorr: Okay, now Raymond Saulnier. President Eisenhower knew a lot about military life; he knew something about politics, I think; but I don't think economics was a strong point. So how did you educate him on economics?

Raymond Saulnier: It's been thirty years now since he left the White House and in those thirty years, I've been asked that question probably 300 times. Did Eisenhower understand economics? I got to be more and more puzzled and sort of frustrated by the question. I finally decided that there was an answer, at least a response, that I could make to it, and the response is: compared to what other President? I thought, did Roosevelt understand economics? Harry Truman, did he understand economics? Then you go down the list. If you look at it in that way, and that's a fair way to look at it, I think you'll concede that he was pretty knowledgeable, in fact, he was very knowledgeable.

Daniel Schorr: Wait a minute. He's not running anymore.

Raymond Saulnier: No. Nor am I.

Daniel Schorr: Tell us a story about...

Raymond Saulnier: Well, a story about him. You know, they say that you don't really understand a foreign language until you can make a joke about it, and the same is true of economics. It is not a foreign language, but it is to some. I remember one time in 1958, we were in a recession and we were doing just what they're doing today, trying to urge the Federal Reserve System to give us a little help. The Fed was reluctant. They usually are. I was there one afternoon talking with him about this. Of course, I had been in contact with Martin, who was running the Fed at the time. I was full of their reasons why nothing much was being done. It was the end of the year, the '57-58 period, winter, and the explanation that the Fed had for why they hadn't acted was that at that time of year it is very difficult to know just what's happening in the financial system. There are flows of currency in and out. It's hard to know what to do until you get out of the holiday period. They couldn't act for us because, as I explained it to him, there was Thanksgiving, and then there was Christmas. Then there was New Year. He listened to the whole thing and he finally said to me, "Do you think we can get this done by Valentine's Day?" Well, what could you say? I said, "Yes, we can try." Now, there isn't very much we could do, but if you look at the record, you'll see that the discount rate was cut, I think, February 13. That's not the point. The point is that he knew enough about economics to rise above this technical story about flows of funds and holidays.

Daniel Schorr: Thank you. Attorney General Brownell. You had to deal with President Eisenhower on important issues, sometimes very controversial issues. You had to take him down south to enforce school desegregation. You had a lot of tough jobs. You can tell any one of those but don't forget to tell how he reacted and how you dealt with him.

Herbert Brownell: Well, Mr. Moderator, that's quite an assignment. I have to add, first, one addendum to Brad Patterson's story about the Cabinet. You were quite right in saying that he was very orderly with the Cabinet. He had a written agenda prepared ahead of time and he insisted that it be followed. But the first thing in every meeting, as requested by the President, there was a moment of silent prayer during which we all bowed our heads.

One day we came into the Cabinet meeting and Eisenhower and Dulles were engaged in vigorous conversation. There had been some crisis in the Middle East as usual and they were very excited about it. We sat down in the Cabinet meeting and the President started talking about this world crisis. He went on for a few minutes and suddenly he slapped his hands to his head and said, "Damn it, I forgot the prayer!" We followed the established practice and had the prayer.

My experiences with him were best characterized by the first assignment that he ever gave me as Attorney General and that was that he delegated to me the analysis of the "pardoning power" which, as you know, is one of the most unlimited powers of our President. He said he would like to have me advise on the pardons and also the death sentences imposed by the military authorities in the Armies of Occupation in Germany and in Korea. I went the first time to present my report to him and I thought I had done a very professional job in analyzing all the details. I started in my best lawyerly fashion, gave the facts in the first case, then the facts in the second case, then the facts in the third case and he stopped me. He said, "Say, Herb, what are you doing to me? I assigned this job to you. Give me your recommendations and I'll accept them." I thought that was great. He signed everything that I asked him to sign. I turned on my heels to go out of the room and he said, "But remember, Herb, if anything goes wrong you're the fellow that did it." I tell that because it was so typical of him. He delegated great authority to his Cabinet members and his advisors but he expected them to measure up and take the responsibility that went with it. He acted that way through all the time that I knew him.

Daniel Schorr: Are we talking about "known" names of persons to be pardoned or just...

Herbert Brownell: He approached the thing this way. Before he became President, when a President pardoned someone, they didn't make it public and so there grew up in the press and in the media, definitely, a suspicion that the President was giving pardons for ulterior purposes, maybe political reasons or something of that sort. The first thing he established was that every time he pardoned a person the name of that person and the background would be given to the media at the time that he gave the pardon. But he asked the media to please not publicize this thing unless they saw some matter of real public importance because the people that he was pardoning had gone back to their home communities and started a new life and to have this publicity come out then that he was pardoning them would probably set them back. All the time he was in office, every time that he pardoned someone, he gave it to the press with that request. It was a very humanitarian thing to do.

Daniel Schorr: Was it observed?

Herbert Brownell: It was observed all the time that I was in office.

Daniel Schorr: Boy, that was when there was a kinder and easier press.

Alright, let's go on. We're still dealing with economic matters first. Turning to Glenn Seaborg: I want to save you for last for a reason.

Seaborg: Save the best for last.

Daniel Schorr: Not the best, but for a reason. *(Turning to Elmer Staats):* Remind this audience which reads now of a $295 billion dollar budget deficit, when you were working on budgets for the President, what kind of numbers were you working on?

Elmer Staats: Well, the numbers, even if we adjusted them for inflation, would be awfully small compared to what they are today. I remember when Eisenhower became President, the Defense budget was under $25 billion.

Eisenhower became deeply involved with the budget, probably not as much as President Truman had because President Truman had been a member of the Senate Appropriations Committee and knew a lot of those figures going back.

Daniel Schorr: How would that express itself? You go in and say, Mr. President, I've got to talk to you about the budget. Then what happens?

Elmer Staats: Well, we had several sessions a week with him actually. The door was always open when we wanted to see him or when he wanted to see us. I served in that position for three years from 1958 to 1961, and in that process, I sat in on all the meetings he had with the Congressional leaders and at the Cabinet meeting and so on. I agree with what Steve [Raymond] Saulnier was saying, he was not only knowledgeable but very much interested. There was a story that went around from the beginning of the Eisenhower administration that he was a victim of two very strong people, one of them was Sherman Adams on the domestic side and the other was Foster Dulles on the international side.

Daniel Schorr: A word of explanation. You're dealing here with another generation. Sherman Adams was the White House Chief of Staff at the time and was obliged to resign as a result of a scandal involving gifts he had received from somebody named Bernard Goldfine. John Foster Dulles was the Secretary of State who died in office, I believe. He pursued a rather vigorous anti-communist policy and perhaps a more aggressive policy sometimes than the President would seem willing to pursue. Go ahead.

Elmer Staats: I wouldn't gainsay the point that those two individuals played an important part but there's another person that played a very important part behind the scenes and that was his brother, Milton, whom I had gotten to know over the years—a very close personal friend of mine. I first learned about Eisenhower through him. I never met President Eisenhower until he became President. But Milton Eisenhower was very sage, down to earth and, of course, deeply loyal to his brother. Undoubtedly, those three people played an important part in Eisenhower's thinking.

The point I'm leading up to is, it seems to me that when Sherman Adams left the White House and Foster Dulles became ill and died, Eisenhower realized that he had to dig more deeply into issues instead of relying on these two individuals. I think I could sense that as I sat through the meetings of the Cabinet and the Congressional leaders. I don't think that Eisenhower would have bought the supply side economics anymore than Steve [Raymond Saulnier] would have bought the supply side economics.

Daniel Schorr: Did such a thing as supply side economics exist in those days?

Elmer Staats: The theory of supply side economics is that if you cut taxes enough you stimulate the economy and more than make up for lost revenues and that has tripled our national debt in around eight years.

Bradley Patterson: Steve [Raymond Saulnier], our colleagues at Brookings used to call those people the "sunshine boys."

Elmer Staats: If I may, I'd like to talk a little about the

National Security Council (NSC). These are obviously related because a lot of the budget issues got resolved in the NSC. When Eisenhower was running for President, he felt deeply that we needed to speak with one voice overseas. When we entered World War II, there was only one agency in the United States Government that had staff located outside the United States and that was the State Department. When the war ended, we had fourteen agencies. They ranged from Treasury, Atomic Energy Commission, Agriculture, and so on. He felt that it was important that we have some better way of relating all of these interests into a national policy. General "Beetle" Smith [William Bedell "Beetle" Smith] had been his Chief of Staff in Europe and had been head of the CIA appointed by President Truman. Allen Dulles had been number two in the CIA and Gordon Gray had been Secretary of the Army. General Robert Cutler, had been a close associate of President Eisenhower's; these four people helped him write two campaign speeches, setting forth a plan where you would take the National Security Council, which had already been established in 1949, and develop a mechanism to do policy planning on a country or a regional basis and then an Operations Coordinating Board of which I was a staff director. He said we should take those policies and plans and put "meat" on them and implement them in concrete, specific terms: foreign aid, military assistance, and so on. Out of this came these two bodies, a policy planning staff and an operations coordinating staff. I cite this partly as a backup for what I think was an important decision that he made in 1953. When the French lost Dien Bien Phu, they asked President Eisenhower to come in with military forces to save what was left of the French troops. A series of task forces were made up of these two bodies, advising him as to what they thought he should do. I remember distinctly a very long briefing in the Cabinet room by the joint chiefs of staff with their maps showing the terrain of Viet Nam; no airfields, lots of jungle, little hamlets and so on, and the joint chiefs said, "Mr. President, we've come to the conclusion that if you went into Viet Nam, there's no chance that you could win unless you were prepared to use nuclear weapons." "Well," he said, "that decides it for me. We will not use nuclear weapons." He turned to Beetle Smith, who was then the Under Secretary of State in the new administration, and said, "Beetle, pack your bags and go to Paris. You've got to negotiate." Now this was a very strongly held view on his part. Nuclear weapons were a very non-viable means of warfare. He would say time after time in our meetings with him, "There is no such thing as limited nuclear war because there will be escalation." I've heard him say this many, many times.

Daniel Schorr: We have to recall that, before President Eisenhower, President Truman at one point, had mentioned the possibility of using nuclear weapons in Korea and thought that was a worthwhile thing. General MacArthur would not have minded using nuclear weapons. Here we have President Eisenhower who, you would think would be the great military leader, wanting to use every weapon that he had, but probably more restrained about nuclear weapons than most of the people around there.

Elmer Staats: I think that is correct. He felt that the nuclear energy was a source for power, for medicine. One of the responsibilities that I had was to try to develop a program for international peaceful uses for atomic energy. That was a way in which we could transfer this technology to other countries with the hope that it would provide a peaceful end use rather than a weapons use.

Daniel Schorr: Yes, and of course for those who have not read that history, in those days President Eisenhower came up with an Atoms for Peace proposal. He made a proposal to the Soviet Union that they meet and pool their energy, their resources, for peaceful purposes and in those days, the Cold War days, it was not possible to reach any agreement with the Soviet Union. With enormous foresight, President Eisenhower had been one of the great advocates of trying to "turn swords into plowshares" in nuclear terms.

Turning to Glenn Seaborg. This was a science advisor to the President who happens to have a certain interest in nuclear weapons, Glenn Seaborg.

Glenn Seaborg: Perhaps I should start by recounting the first close contact I had with President Eisenhower and that was before I became a member of the President's Science Advisory Committee, when my wife, Helen, and I were invited to a dinner at the White House. Now, that's quite a distance to come to dinner; to travel from San Francisco to Washington, D.C., but we thought that it was probably worth doing. I remember that after the dinner, the ladies retired with Mrs. Eisenhower to the Red Room and the gentlemen retired to the Green Room with President Eisenhower, that was for coffee and liqueurs and...

Daniel Schorr: ...and cigars?

Glenn Seaborg: Well, cigars and cigarettes in the case of the gentlemen and cigarettes in the case of the ladies. What I remember in this first contact, which was before I became a member of the President's Science Advisory Committee, was how personable and approachable President Eisenhower was. This was early in 1958, shortly after Sputnik. Sputnik was the first launch of a space satellite in orbit around the earth by the Russians. They beat us to it and caught us by surprise. That, of course, was the topic of conversation in the Green Room. We had just launched our first space satellite into orbit. This was a few months after the Russians succeeded in doing theirs. I remember how interested President Eisenhower was in this maneuver and how glad he was that we had been able to achieve this success. The conversation went on then to a broader discussion of the importance of science and technology to our country in today's highly competitive, high technology world. I was impressed by how interested he was in this subject and, in many respects, how knowledgeable he was.

Daniel Schorr: Do you recall a specific thing you discussed with him and a specific thing he said?

Glenn Seaborg: I would have to jump to a later meeting with him when I recall vividly a specific thing he talked about and that was arms limitation. He was very concerned about the potentially devastating role of nuclear weapons and had almost a fixation in his desire that we should somehow be able to negotiate a test ban with the Soviet Union. He would have preferred a comprehensive test ban but, as things developed, he began to see that perhaps it would have to be a limited test ban, that is a ban on testing in the atmosphere but one that still allowed testing underground. I was very much impressed by how completely devoted to that objective he was and sometimes I wish that perhaps...

Elmer Staats: A footnote to what Glenn has said. One of the concerns in that period was the Soviets using the Antarctic as a base for military operations and possibly nuclear weapons. We took the initiative in developing an Antarctic Peace Treaty, a peaceful agreement that the Antarctic would be used for peaceful scientific purposes and to ban all weapons or weapons-type operations there. And that still prevails today.

Glenn Seaborg: Yes, that's one of the treaties.

Herbert Brownell: I could add something there and I'd like to, if I may, about his attitude about the use of the atomic bomb. When he was elected and before he was inaugurated, he carried out his campaign promise to go to Korea. The war was daily producing many casualties for the American forces that were in Korea and the people were disturbed about that. He went to Korea personally and received the advice of all the military people there, on the ground. Our American generals urged him to wage an all out war even if it was necessary to invade China. He talked to General MacArthur, who gave him the same advice. They said that if the Chinese turned against us we could use the atomic bomb. That was at a time when the United States was the only country that had the atomic bomb, or so we thought. This was in early 1953. He received unanimous advice from his military advisors that they should wage all out war in Korea and, if necessary, in China and, if necessary, use the atomic bomb. He kept his own counsel. When he came back from Korea, he made his decision and that was that he would not use the atomic bomb to end that war; rather, he entered into negotiations and, as you remember, during the first year of his first term he settled the Korean War without further bloodshed and kept the peace for the balance of his eight years in office. To me, his approach to these world problems was very illuminating. Even though we had the power, he decided against using the bomb.

Glenn Seaborg: I agree. We actually didn't have a complete monopoly. The Russians had exploded an atomic bomb in August of 1949, but we had rather decisive superiority at that time.

Herbert Brownell: That's right.

Daniel Schorr: Let me bring us back to something a little bit more personal. Let me ask any or all of you, now it can be told after all these years, in your dealings with President Eisenhower, did he ever get mad at you. If so, how did he act when he was angry?

Elmer Staats: I don't think I ever saw him get mad at anybody in a sense of "venting his spleen," in the same way that

Lyndon Johnson did. I think he got irritated once with General Cutler. Cutler was briefing the Security Council on issues and he finally said, "Bobby, quit briefing us. Bring us some problems here that we can resolve." He was pretty agitated about it. But that's about the nearest example of being angry that I can give.

Raymond Saulnier: I think this is one of the features of the man where understanding has been wrong. I had seen him many times, frustrated; I've seen him irritated, impatient with things that he'd have to go through that were needlessly long, needlessly complex, but I'd never seen him angry; I'd never seen him mad. There was nothing irascible about him, yet there is a reputation that somehow he'd get "red headed" and get terribly worked up. Now, maybe it happened, but not to my knowledge. That was not an aspect of the man that was known to me.

Daniel Schorr: How lucky you are. Anybody else? Or is that question leading to a dry hole?

Elmer Staats: Well, I heard him get pretty excited. He had been to an international conference in Paris and de Gaulle dismissed himself and left Eisenhower there at the table because de Gaulle was then Head of Government. Eisenhower had had a long relationship with de Gaulle anyway, but it was not a very favorable one and he was terribly excited about it. He said, "Why can't we reorganize our government so that when I go into a conference like this, I don't suffer that kind of an embarrassment."

Bradley Patterson: I remember once, and Mr. Brownell you also might remember, in a Cabinet meeting where I think we were discussing a civil rights bill. We had come to a conclusion and Eisenhower said, "We're going to do this and here's the policy and now we'll send it to Congress." Then he stopped and added, "That's like throwing pearls before certain animals."

Herbert Brownell: I saw him madder than that.

Daniel Schorr: All right, now we're getting down to it.

Herbert Brownell: But personally, not at me. The maddest I ever saw him get after he was President was at Senator Joe McCarthy. McCarthy started to investigate the Army, acting without evidence, making charges loosely and damaging peoples' reputations. He had called Eisenhower a communist, among others, but he started calling these generals in the Army communists and several of them had served under...

Daniel Schorr: Among others, Secretary of the Army Stevens, was damaged by McCarthy, General Marshall was maligned by McCarthy...

Herbert Brownell: Yes, and you remember several of the generals at Monmouth of New Jersey, and people who had served with Eisenhower; several of whom he knew personally to be very upstanding, loyal Americans. I saw him completely lose his temper on that occasion. He said to me, "We've got to stop this."

Daniel Schorr: Wow, that's pretty wild!

Herbert Brownell: He said, "We've got to find some way to stop him. You can't tell me that I have to serve up these members of the Army to his investigations." So, I gave him an opinion, starting with George Washington, and almost every President down the line. Whenever the Congress served subpoenas that actually interfered with and prevented the Executive Branch from carrying out their duties, Presidents have refused to honor the subpoenas. He acted on that and he issued an order that no member of the Executive Branch was required, and in fact was forbidden, to respond to these subpoenas from the McCarthy investigating committee. That broke the back of McCarthyism because it was the fodder that McCarthy lived on. Get these people up there, one after the other, call them communists, rage at them and insult them in various ways. That chopped it right off. McCarthy had no more fodder. No more representatives from the Executive Branch appeared before his committee.

Daniel Schorr: Indulge me, General, in this question which, to this day, interests me. In those days, he was telling you, you had to cut out whatever expletives you were deleting at that point. I was watching him at press conferences and at those press conferences we could not get him to offer any personal criticism of McCarthy. Nor, in fact, even to go very far in giving personal defenses of people that McCarthy was attacking. Now, if I recall, President Eisenhower went to Wisconsin for a campaign speech. I'm told that he dropped a couple of paragraphs defending General Marshall out of his speech because he was in McCarthy's home state. How was it possible that he could be so mild-mannered in public where as you indicate, he was so indignant in private?

Herbert Brownell: There is an explanation for that. It never has gotten across satisfactorily in my opinion. McCarthy was head of the Senate Investigating Committee and he had complete power to continue his hearings so long as the Senate backed him up. The President couldn't fire McCarthy. McCarthy was an elected Senator. He watched Truman's actions vis a vis McCarthy. Truman engaged in a real cat and dog fight with McCarthy and that turned out, in Eisenhower's opinion, to be the wrong tactics because it built up McCarthy. McCarthy was running for President and he was delighted to have the publicity. So that didn't work. Eisenhower did act differently in public than he did in private about the McCarthy matter and he waited until the decisive moment came when he could act within his authority as President and chop off any further hearings. That was so typical of his way of doing business.

Daniel Schorr: You may recall that as "chopping off the hearings." I covered those hearings. I don't recall they were quite so decisively chopped off. I don't recall that McCarthy was *really* chopped off until after Ed Murrow did an hour long program showing what McCarthy was really like, and then the conservatives in the Senate began to gang up on McCarthy. That's when I thought that he [President Eisenhower] was not helping the Republican cause very much.

Herbert Brownell: That was a complementary action. Murrow was wonderful in that and his broadcast had a great deal of effect on public opinion toward McCarthy. The Senate itself, about that time, got fed up with McCarthy and appointed a Special Investigative Committee and they finally censured him. Eisenhower called the Chairman of that Committee, Senator Watkins, into the White House, praised him for it publicly and had his picture taken with him. Those two actions, one from the President and one from the Senate itself converged almost in the same month and put an end to the whole era.

Daniel Schorr: I could spend a whole night with you on this alone but I think that would be self-indulgence. Do any of you want to add to this before I go to our participants out there who may have questions? Yes, Raymond.

Raymond Saulnier: I was going to say that it was a policy with him [Eisenhower] that he did not attack individuals in public. I've had occasion to look pretty carefully at the whole range of his papers, his *public* papers; and you won't find attacks on people in them—I mean how he'd feel about them. He had his ideas. He had very strong feelings. It was a matter of principle with him—a tactic that I'm sure he thought was the right way to handle people.

Daniel Schorr: Time and time again, he would say at press conferences and on public occasions, "I will not attack any one person or his motives." It would be a principle of his that he did not deliver personal attacks, although many richly deserved them.

Elmer Staats: Dan, I think a word might be said about Eisenhower as a good listener. Brad, I think, testified to this in his role in the Cabinet. I remember once a meeting of the Security Council where we were discussing some major issue (I've forgotten now what the specifics were, that's not important). Eisenhower got to Wilson, who was Secretary of Defense, and said, "Well, now, what does your staff think about this point?" Wilson reared back and said, "In General Motors, I was paid $250,000 a year to do the thinking." That's the difference between the two people. Eisenhower wanted to listen to see what his staff thought before he made up his mind but it was also a pretty good insight on Wilson.

Daniel Schorr: Just my last question, then we're going to go out there, but it follows what you've said. In regard to the other reputation that President Eisenhower has had, and it may be inside the beltway, and I'm not sure we *had* a beltway, but it was the fact that from his military background he liked using the staff system, delegated an awful lot and frequently allowed Cabinet members and staff to go on automatic pilot for a long, long time without becoming personally involved in many, many decisions. Is that right?

Herbert Brownell: That's exactly right.

Bradley Patterson: Not to my knowledge.

Herbert Brownell: He delegated very broad powers to his advisors, especially in the Cabinet. He knew what they were doing and he would caution them at various times not to go too far but he always knew what was going on. He gave them responsibility perhaps beyond any Cabinet since that time.

Glenn Seaborg: Let me give a little vignette on the other side. While I was serving as a member of the President's Science Advisory Committee, I was the chairman of a subcommittee that studied the relationship between scientific research and graduate education and the Federal government and the universities. We came out with that report, "Scientific Progress, the Universities and the Federal Government," near the end of President Eisenhower's term. He was so interested that he actually took a copy of this report, edited it and made some changes in it. It was a report, of course, that finally had an impact on the role of the Federal Government in supporting scientific research and graduate education.

Bradley Patterson: Dan, we don't want to go too far on this "delegation" bit because I remember, in 1956—and Steve [Raymond Saulnier] may remember—he set up an alerting process called "Staff Notes." This was where he required every Cabinet officer to send him, every evening, anticipatory information on important events or decisions about to be made, matters about to happen and problems just over the horizon. At first, General Goodpaster and his staff had to fight very, very hard to get the Cabinet to understand what "anticipatory information" was; they much preferred to tell him, "everyone's happy, the sun is shining, the flowers are blooming," and so forth. But he insisted on this. In the end, 9,600 items were sent in and 7,500 of them were put into this little daily brief for him, so that he kept his fingers, very quietly, on lots of things that were happening.

Daniel Schorr: Did he ever change a decision at the last minute?

Bradley Patterson: Many times he would scratch on the margin, (and I have a sample copy in my briefcase), "What about this?" and demand more information.

Incidentally, the audience might be interested in seeing the reaction of the press at the very beginning in the Fall of 1954, when the Cabinet and the Staff Secretariat were first established. The *Washington Daily News* tried to scare the people by putting out the headline [holds up a copy of the October 21, 1954, page one] that Eisenhower was just an old military man and was trying to organize his White House like an encampment. That was an overstatement, of course, Dan, an overstatement by the press. Have you ever heard anything like that?

Daniel Schorr: An overstatement by the press? Give me a week, I might think of one.

Let us go now to the audience who have been very patient while all these old fogies, including me, sit around here and reminisce about a kinder and gentler time in this country.

Herbert Parmet: My name is Herbert Parmet and I guess my question would probably be directed to General Brownell and possibly several others. I've struggled with this question of Eisenhower and McCarthy for over twenty years and I find myself being less and less persuaded. There was a matter of strategy in bringing down McCarthy rather than a heavy dosage of political expediency. I wonder sometimes what would have happened if McCarthy had not been stupid enough to take on the Army; but, to get down to my question. You're perfectly right. Eisenhower did not want to attack individuals in public and I agree with you. He knew very well, and we have it in his correspondence, that to attack McCarthy in public would be to give him the kind of prominence that the Senator wanted. What nags me are, in addition to the kind of things that Mr. Schorr pointed out, some simple matters; for example, in June of 1953, Eisenhower went to Dartmouth and at that commencement, he suddenly added a paragraph on to his speech advising the graduates, don't join the book burners. The press immediately assumed that he was talking about McCarthy because Cohn and Schine were examining the overseas libraries. McCarthy quipped as a result, "Well, I've never burned any books." At any rate, at the very next press conference, Eisenhower was asked whether he had been talking about McCarthy. Now, you see, it wasn't a matter now of getting personal about McCarthy; but what Eisenhower said was, in his dissembling way, "I wouldn't want my students to read any of those Marxist books myself." He was joining McCarthy in that without mentioning McCarthy and, far from repudiating McCarthy he was conveying McCarthy's sense of intellectual censorship. Was that strategy for bringing down McCarthy? I'm not convinced. That is the question. I just see it as part of the whole thing.

Daniel Schorr: Let me briefly summarize the question. I remember those press conferences also and it has to do with the fact that it was true there were two staff members of McCarthy's, Cohn and Schine, dropping around Europe, making quite a scene, pulling books out of USIA libraries, where in certain cases it was certainly outrageous. At a press conference, Eisenhower said he was against book burning; that was taken to be a criticism of those tactics. Later on, at another press conference he indeed said that he would not favor reading all these Marxists books. On the other hand he also said, and it was contradictory, "We really have to read these people to know who the enemy is." The fact of the matter is that he did leave a certain cloud of doubt as to whether or not he was unqualifiedly against censorship of books in U.S. libraries overseas.

Herbert Brownell: I think that's a fair statement. His press conferences on that subject were not clear to the public. What he was trying to do, I know, was to speak on the principle of whether or not there should be censorship of books in government libraries; and on that I thought he was quite clear. But he would not take the other road which was to attack McCarthy. In his own mind, on the one hand he drew a distinction between commenting on the principle of an important matter like censorship of books in government libraries; on the other hand was the advisability of making a personal attack on McCarthy. That was the line he tried to draw and, as sometimes happens even to some of the rest of us, we don't always quite get the point across.

Daniel Schorr: Okay, next question.

Bob Krone: I'm Bob Krone from the University of Southern California. My question is a general one. If Ike were President today, how would he deal with Saddam Hussein and the situation in the Middle East?

Daniel Schorr: I guess the closest thing we have to a foreign expert is somebody who served on the National Security Council. The question is the same question that came up during the press conference. It is, if President Eisenhower were President today, how would he deal with Saddam Hussein in Iraq?

Elmer Staats: Well, I wouldn't want to really venture speculation on that at all. I have my own ideas but that's irrelevant.

Daniel Schorr: Well, he can't get at you now.

Elmer Staats: I think it's a no win situation and I think it would probably be a no win situation for any President. If there would be a question in my mind as to what he might have done, and I say it would be pure speculation, it's whether he would have gone beyond the question of defending Saudi Arabia. That would be my question. I think that he might have tried to negotiate some.

But I think it would be pretty hard to fault what Bush has done with respect to utilizing the UN. The UN is a different body today now than before Iraq. I think that Eisenhower would have used the UN much the same way that Bush has. If there's any doubt in my mind on the question of whether he'd gone beyond defending Kuwait and Saudi Arabia...

Daniel Schorr: Does this remind you of the current cooperation in the United Nations with the Soviet Union which people call unprecedented? Does it remind you of 1956, when the Soviet Union and the United States teamed up to tell the French, British and Israelis to get out of Suez?

Elmer Staats: Well, that's correct. You make a good point. It slipped my mind. Yes, that's right.

Daniel Schorr: Okay, next question.

Tom Wolfe: Mr. Schorr, my name's Tom Wolfe, and I'm a trustee of the Eisenhower Society, co-sponsors of this event this week. I first worked for President Eisenhower during the 1952 campaign in New York and, subsequently, for various administrations. I got to know Sherman Adams very slightly, I was very young then. Mr. Schorr mentioned the vicuna coat that Bernard Goldfine of Scarsdale, New York, gave to Sherman Adams, and thereafter Adams departed from the White House. To my memory, that was one of the earliest scandals of which we have so many in administrations more recently. I wondered whether, with all your wonderful memories up there, you can remember some other situations that occurred and how President Eisenhower dealt with those. As I remember, Mr. Adams left very quietly and went back to New Hampshire and there wasn't all this investigation and argument and pleading, "Well I didn't really mean to do that, I didn't do anything wrong and you should keep me on," and so on. There was an effort to make things as easy as possible for the President. I just wondered whether you would talk about how President Eisenhower handled other situations like that if there were any others of that nature. There may not have been any others.

Daniel Schorr: It's an interesting question. Have you heard the question? It is how did he respond, how did he, as a person with such rectitude himself, deal with impropriety when he discovered it among the people who worked with him?

Bradley Patterson: Well, Tom, I might amplify one thing.

There *was* some mish mash about Adams' resignation. There were hearings and he testified before the hearings. Sherm's mistake was that he had made an inquiry to the Federal Trade Commission about Goldfine's case and that, of course, is something that no White House officer ever does—call any regulatory commission. Incidentally, any of us would have been fired immediately if we had done that kind of thing because you *just don't contact regulatory commissions about their business.* Adams had done it in an innocent way. Goldfine had been somebody who had contributed a great deal to the economy of New Hampshire when Adams was governor. He felt he was an old friend; a close personal friend. There were hearings and a big mish mash about it. Eisenhower's first reaction about Adams' mistake was, "I need him, I don't want to see him go," but the elections of '58 were coming and the Republicans on the Hill persuaded him that he had to let him go, which was a very painful thing for both of them.

Daniel Schorr: You're saying something very interesting. You're saying that he wasn't shocked, scandalized, but that it was a matter of expediency to let Sherman Adams go.

Bradley Patterson: Yes, he was under political pressure in 1958 to do that. Now, remember Jimmy Carter and Burt Lance. Carter wanted to hold onto Burt Lance. There are many examples of Presidents who have close friends and don't want to let them go, no matter what they are accused of. It was very tough for the President; there was televised testimony and Adams tried to defend himself but he had to leave.

Raymond Saulnier: Incidentally, it was not a coat. It was a bolt of cloth.

Bradley Patterson: It was a rug.

Raymond Saulnier: Well, there was a rug involved also.

Daniel Schorr: Vicuna cloth?

Raymond Saulnier: Yes, it was a bolt of cloth.

Daniel Schorr: Made of vicuna?

Raymond Saulnier: As the story has been told and retold, it has been transformed. It got to be a coat, it got to be a more elaborate coat but it started out as a bolt of cloth.

Daniel Schorr: Was the word "vicuna" correct?

Raymond Saulnier: Yes. There was a close family friendship between the Goldfines and the Adams'. It arose from the fact that when Adams was governor of New Hampshire in the 1930's, the state was in terrible shape. The mills up there were out of business and Goldfine came into New Hampshire. He would take over one of these factories, refurbish it, install machinery, get a business going and the first thing you knew, there were fifty or a hundred people who had jobs in this community. If you know New Hampshire, it's a land of little valleys with a town in the middle of them. If the mill had a hundred people working, they were in business. Now, Adams was just completely grateful for what Goldfine had done and so it became a very close family connection. When Adams came to Washington, my guess is they had a house in the Rock Creek area and it was probably larger than they had in New Hampshire. Goldfine told them, "Look we've got some rugs in the warehouse that we're not using," one of them was brought out and it was loaned to them for the living room or one of the rooms. As it developed, all of this had a certain element of naivete in it, talking to the Federal Trade Commission on a matter that had to do with the labeling of cotton shirts that Goldfine was making. Adams shouldn't have done that. He was naive to have done that. But the rest was simple acts of friendship between two families that had been friends for a long time and were fond of one another.

Bradley Patterson: It illustrates the very tight ethical standards that everybody in the White House staff has to live under, almost too tight, almost cruel, but nonetheless, very much the fact that you simply do not even give the *appearance* of accepting favors or having your judgment altered. Incidentally, Mrs. Patterson reminded me of the end of the story. Mrs. Adams very graciously would have the White House wives into the Adams house for luncheons or for teas. The wives were often neglected and had their family lives just miserably disrupted by their husbands' continued activity at the White House. At one particular luncheon, she was serving coffee and she reminded all her White House guests, "Don't spill any coffee on *that* rug."

Daniel Schorr: Well, the good news is that the White House is back in the hands of a New Hampshire governor.

George Wills: My name is George Wills and I worked for a number of years for Milton Eisenhower. My question is, in light of all that has occurred in the last several days with Congress, with the relationship of the President to the Congress and the problems in establishing a budget and making decisions and also recognizing that he had a Democratically-controlled Congress, Johnson and Rayburn, and the negotiations that obviously had to take place on fundamental, financial questions, how would President Eisenhower have led and directed and given leadership the last week with what we faced in this country with the budget?

Daniel Schorr: The question as you've heard, really bears on one of the most important sides of President Eisenhower and that is the coalition-building side. The question is, if President Eisenhower were dealing with the Democratic Congress as President Bush is today, if he had to deal, well he had to deal with one House of congressional Democrats for awhile, but if he were dealing with a Democratic Congress, would he summon from his coalition-building talents and techniques, to deal with that Congress and compromise and make plans with them better than what has been happening in recent years?

Raymond Saulnier: I don't know. The whole situation is so totally different from anything that existed in the Eisenhower period. It's hard for me to visualize or to speculate on what he might do in the situation. Here we have a budget that's nearly $300 billion out of whack. Now, what would he do in such a situation? Well, I'm tempted to say he wouldn't have gotten into it. But what you do when you're there is another matter.

Daniel Schorr: Well, you're considering the question too broadly. Clearly, with a $295 billion budget deficit, if you start from there, there are no quick and easy ways to do it. I think the question was a more general question of the way that President Eisenhower would deal with people not of his party, and his way of getting along with disparate groups of people.

Raymond Saulnier: Well, the methods that have been followed are not his.

Daniel Schorr: I was handing that to you. Alright, maybe somebody else.

Bradley Patterson: I think one answer to your question as Steve was saying, is the difference in the Congress today. Lyndon Johnson and Sam Rayburn could deliver the votes, and you wouldn't have a Newt Gingrich walking off 180 degrees in the other direction.

Elmer Staats: Your question is a very good question, but let me preface what I'm going to say by saying it's a very different Congress today than it was when Eisenhower was President. You have a proliferation of subcommittees. Members of Congress have very little loyalty toward their party leadership, everyone's on their own and they're out for P.A.C. money and they're going to get re-elected. It's a *very different* kind of a Congress today than we had. Having said that, I think what I said about Eisenhower being a good listener carried over into his relations to Congress. I sat in on Congressional leaders' meetings quite regularly. He not only had his own party leaders there but there were many meetings where he brought in the opposition as well. I think he recognized that by not having served in Congress himself, he wanted to defer to people like Lyndon Johnson and Everett Dirkson and Sam Rayburn. Now, I think he was able to put together coalitions that way and that he did it in a quiet way. He didn't go on the TV and blast the Congress, so much of what we hear today. I think he wanted to work behind the scenes. He also had two very able liaison people who had a lot of experience on the Hill, General Jerry Persons, who had been the legislative liaison for the Air Force and Bryce Harlow who served on the Armed Services Committee Staff. I think all these things together made for a very effective relationship and he was able to accomplish a lot of things but it's still a very different Congress today and it's very hard to know how it would work today.

Daniel Schorr: Okay, my own theory is that they were all Texans, Johnson and Rayburn; and when Eisenhower and these Texans got together they thought they could do things.

Are we finished? All right, two more questions. I want to have a small summary statement from these people before they go so think up the last word you want to say after these questions.

President Gordon Haaland: Gordon Haaland, from Gettysburg College. During his tenure as President, President Eisenhower was criticized for not being, or not appearing to be, in charge, as you've testified even this evening. He delegated a good deal of authority to his Cabinet and to other people and he had two powerful public figures in Adams and Foster Dulles. Yet, in recent years clearly, and your own testimony suggests, he was very much involved with the government, very much in terms of his own self in charge. Two questions really: Did he ever lament or was he concerned about the criticisms of his style of leadership? Did he respond privately to the public criticisms that were offered at that time, to his style of leadership; and did he ever consider changing it, that is to say, taking more public responsibility for some of the actions of his government?

Daniel Schorr: Let's face it. We can say it now after all these years. In those days, people said that he was lazy, played a lot of golf, left it to you people to run the government, wasn't around there much of the time, his smile was loose, relaxed. That was what was being said then. The question was, did he resent that kind of criticism? Did it roll off of him?

Bradley Patterson: Well, he may have resented the criticism. You used the word "lament." Did he ever lament; and the answer is "no." In fact, he stood up very strongly. There's a press conference quote—[April 2, 1958]—where he's asked about the White House staff, the kind of thing I held up for you. He got right up there and said, in effect, "The White House staff is an important part of my administration and any good commander has to have a staff; but they don't make the decisions, I make the decisions." It was a very strong statement of defense in the end; and the quote appears in the little commemorative book that we put out about the White House. So, no, he did not lament. He got right up there and defended his system of administration.

Raymond Saulnier: I have no recollection of him agonizing about such things. I don't think it meant a thing to him. He was interested in what should be done in a situation but if somebody out there didn't like it, it was not really something that got under his skin. He paid little attention to it. You will find in just about the last of his press conferences, that he was asked about what he thought would be his place in history, a rather presumptuous question; and he said as a response to that, "That will be determined by the historians." Directly after that, he ended up 25th in the list of Presidents in a poll of historians. Well, it has been left to the historians, and by and large his record improves.

Daniel Schorr: There is no question that he's gone up in the polls since retirement from the presidency about as fast as the recent President has gone down.

Bradley Patterson: Dan, I can add one thing. You remember the U-2 affair. The beginning was a cover statement that this was a weather plane and so forth; and there was no White House responsibility. But in the end, Eisenhower announced that it *was* his responsibility; that *he* had made the decision, and the papers jumped on him—you probably did too, Dan.

Daniel Schorr: Me? Never!

Bradley Patterson: Yes, you.

Daniel Schorr: I still think it was a bad decision by the way.

Bradley Patterson: He opened himself up to that by saying that it was a weather plane and nobody knew anything about it and so forth. Then he came right out and said this was something that was "a decision of mine." I remember him saying to the Cabinet, "Look, if I go on with the theory, the myth, that this is 'plausible deniability,' that this is something that I didn't know anything about, everybody is going to say that I was 'out playing golf' and wasn't running my government and I'm not going to do that, I'm going to take responsibility."

Daniel Schorr: Oh, then he *was* sensitive about that?

Bradley Patterson: Oh, yes. In that case, he was.

Daniel Schorr: Oh, then he *was* sensitive about the golf playing business.

Bradley Patterson: Well, no, he didn't mention golf but he did mention the accusation that he wasn't in charge and, therefore, he took a step which many professionals in the intelligence business believe was a mistake; namely, he had admitted responsibility for an important covert intelligence operation. I think it was the right thing myself.

Daniel Schorr: You do? I'll see you later.

Bradley Patterson: But he did it and he explained it to the Cabinet in that fashion.

Daniel Schorr: Okay, let me just briefly say, and this is another whole discussion, that I was serving in the Soviet Union during that period and I knew Nikita Khrushchev pretty well, as much as foreigners could get to know him. It was devastating to him, not that the U-2 had been flown and shot down over the Soviet Union but that, instead of saying, "Gee, I don't know, my covert action people must have done it," making it possible for them to continue their dialogue, President Eisenhower finally said, after trying a cover story, that he had ordered it. And that made it impossible for Khrushchev to go to his Polit Bureau and say, "I still want to talk to this guy." There are things which Presidents should not take responsibility for.

Bradley Patterson: I disagree.

Daniel Schorr: I know.

Herbert Parmet: My name is Herbert Parmet of the City University of New York. My question is for Mr. Staats, and it really is an attempt to clarify history here. It pertains to what you said about Eisenhower and his attitude toward nuclear weapons. Conventional wisdom, indeed it appears and reappears in many different sources, is that Eisenhower conveyed to the People's Republic of China by way of Harold Stassen to Prime Minister Nehru of India, that we were indeed prepared to use the atomic bomb if necessary in order to bring about an armistice to get those two off to Panmunjom and moving toward fruition. That's one act. In addition to that, we have a much more recent bit of declassified material in an article and then a book, about a young historian named Gordon Chang, which reveals that Eisenhower attempted to make an agreement with Chiang Kai-shek that, if Chiang Kai-shek would remove his troops from Quemoy and Matsu, which as he saw, could only be productive with a great deal of difficulty, Eisenhower was prepared to fill that breech by protecting the islands with nuclear power. We have, therefore, two things here. One that you've heard of, Mr. Staats, certainly, the old conventional one; and now a new one which indicates a willingness, and I won't say 'happiness' to use it, but certainly not an extreme reluctance. Does that do very much to upset your own analysis of the President and nuclear energy?

Daniel Schorr: Just before your answer. Does everybody know about Quemoy and Matsu? Anybody needs to be filled in on those two small islands off the coast of China that were a source of contention between Communist China and China in Formosa for a long time and that Secretary Dulles was issuing threats as to what would happen if the Chinese Communists came in? Go ahead.

Elmer Staats: I'm not sure that I got the full thrust of the whole question to be quite honest with you. It's my fault. My ears are worse than I thought.

Raymond Saulnier: This is not my area, but I do want to say this. Certainly it is my understanding of him from what association I had with him under his presidency and from reading his papers, that he was very, very cautious about the use of nuclear power; that he was really very conservative on that issue. There were others who weren't conservative at all, but not Eisenhower. I hope that, in the historical studies which are being made, it doesn't happen that somebody will pick out an incident in which something was said to Harold Stassen, on some fugitive memorandum and make a theory out of it. Suddenly I'll be told Eisenhower was a nuclear "lone ranger," ready to use the bomb at the slightest provocation, but that is not true.

Elmer Staats: As the question relates solely to the Quemoy, Matsu issue, I was involved in that. We had a group monitoring that situation.

Daniel Schorr: But the question was, did President Eisenhower try to engage Chiang Kai-shek in a specific resolution of the problem of Quemoy and Matsu

Elmer Staats: Yes, but at the same time there was always the uncertainty in intelligence as to what the mainland Chinese were going to do. After all, you're talking about a very short distance there. There were all kinds of contingency plans as to how we would react, what kind of support would we give to Taiwan. My recollection is that there was never any discussion about using nuclear weapons.

Daniel Schorr: I want to thank these marvelous panelists who have come a long way, mainly, I think, because they feel they owe it to you but more, I think, they owe it to the memory of President Eisenhower to be here and try to re-create for you a time not easy to re-create. Nobody can tell you what it was like, for example, actually being able to read your documents without looking up at either C-Span or CNN to know what else was going on. I mean those early primitive days when people still dealt with written things and went into each other's offices to talk to them.

I only want to add one thing that I think we would all agree with. We don't all agree on everything. The U-2 we've got to fight out yet, but one thing I think we will all agree about is, of all the President's whom I've covered, been in any contact with (and they go back to Truman), I would imagine that President Eisenhower had the greatest inner security of any of the President's I've known. And because he had inner security, he transmitted a sense of national security to the American people.

CHAPTER TWO

Eisenhower and the Media

The Eisenhower Symposium at Gettysburg provided, for the first time since the Eisenhower administration left office, an opportunity for members of the press to gather to provide their assessment of the eight years of the Eisenhower presidency. Included on the media panel were the White House correspondents for each of the three major television networks (NBC, ABC, and CBS) and the chief political correspondents from a major east coast (Baltimore) and west coast (Los Angeles) newspaper. In addition, President Reagan's Director of Communications joined the panel to provide a degree of perspective on presidential management of the press and changes since the Eisenhower administration. The moderator of the panel was Stephen Hess, a senior fellow at the Brookings Institution, who served as a speechwriter in the Eisenhower White House and currently writes prodigiously on the presidency.

One of the most striking features of this session is the personal relationship that each of the White House correspondents had with President Eisenhower. Robert Donovan talks about the numerous times he met personally with the President, including a fishing trip in Denver in the summer of 1954.

President Eisenhower, unlike many presidents, was quite comfortable with the press and held frequent press conferences. As Daniel Schorr notes, the President was "not afraid to face the press as some of his recent successors were." President Eisenhower would directly answer questions, and if he didn't know the answer, ask his press secretary, Jim Hagerty, to find the answer. He was the first president to allow reporters to tape his answers, and to hold frequent one-on-one interviews with the press.

Eisenhower's relationship with the press was so strong that

he set up regular news conferences. It is important to remember that one of the legacies of the Eisenhower presidency is that the presidential news conference was institutionalized. Prior to President Eisenhower, reporters did not have a regular mechanism for meeting with the president.

For example, President Roosevelt brought reporters into the Oval Office whenever he wanted to make a point, they stood around his desk, and he told them what he wanted to know. It was not a question and answer session as we know today of press interviews. However, President Eisenhower restructured the relationship of the President to the press by holding press conferences in the White House in the new press room and allowing reporters not only to quote him directly but to tape record him.

President Eisenhower's commitment to expanding the way the press covered the presidency included not only the print media but also television. Although television was not widely available when President Truman left office, Jim Hagerty urged President Eisenhower to use this emerging technology. As Tom Dewey's press secretary in his 1950 run for governor of New York, Hagerty had successfully used television to bolster the campaign. He saw television as an important tool for communicating directly with the public. As a result, Eisenhower was the first President to allow television cameras into the White House. In 1955 the first televised press conferences were held and President Eisenhower stood for a half hour under hot lights to answer reporters questions.

The new relationship with the press that emerged during the Eisenhower years gave rise to not only an institutionalized press conference, but a new position in the White House called the Press Secretary. James Hagerty, who became the first official Press Secretary to a President, subsequently hired a staff to help the President manage the press. This began a new era, in which Presidents not only reported to the American public through the press but began to manage what news was reported and when.

This session brings together an extraordinary group of newsmen who covered the Eisenhower presidency.

PANEL

Moderator: **Stephen Hess,** *Brookings Institution*

Panelists:

Martin Agronsky	*NBC, ABC and CBS News, 1952-69*
Charles Corddry	*Baltimore* Sun
Robert Donovan	*Washington Bureau Chief, Los Angeles* Times
Thomas C. Griscom	*Assistant to the President for Communications, 1987-88*
Andy Rooney	*CBS News, 1959 - present*
Ray Scherer	*NBC News White House Correspondent, 1950-69*
Daniel Schorr	*CBS News, 1953-76*

Stephen Hess: It is very difficult to understand how truly pleased and grateful I am to be up here today unless you know that this grey-haired person was once the baby of President Eisenhower's White House staff. I was 26 when I joined it, and, in fact, last night Fred Greenstein told me that when he was researching the "Hidden Hand Presidency," he found Sherman Adams' oral history. And when he went in it, the interviewer had asked him to assess the leading lights of the administration: the Cabinet, the National Security Council, the staff. And finally he asked Governor Adams "and Steve Hess?" and Adams said, "Now you're scraping the barrel." I had been drafted into the Army in 1956, and got out of the Army as a private first class on Friday of Labor Day weekend in 1958, and on Tuesday, I started as the President's number two speech writer and, as a White House Staff person, was entitled to a sergeant as a driver. Now, if you ever want a definition of real heaven, it's a private first class who's got a sergeant as his driver. I always say that I was the number two speech writer because in this day when George Bush has eight that sounds very grand; but in fact, President Eisenhower had only two. I was there because while I had been in the Army my mentor at Johns Hopkins, Malcolm Moos, became the speech writer to the President and he asked me to join him. The moral of that story for the students in the audience is that you must always be very nice to your professors—you never know when they're going to be in high office.

President Eisenhower had a favorite cartoon from the old *Saturday Evening Post*. It showed a man at a lectern, and he was saying, "Our next speaker needs all the introduction he can get." I truly have been given a panel that needs no introduction but, nevertheless, I'll give a little bit of one and do it in alphabetical order.

A for Agronsky. Martin Agronsky was a combat war correspondent in World War II for NBC, first with the British in Libya in the Middle East and then for the last two years of the war in the Pacific. He was at one point in his illustrious career, the Washington end of the *Today Show*. During at least part of the Eisenhower Administration, he was in Washington as the fellow who opened the ABC radio network every morning at 8:15 weekdays with his commentary. And, of course, you all remember him later for *Agronsky and Company*, the program that really was the pacesetter, the model, for that popular form that now brings us weekend pronouncements from the journalists of Washington.

C would be for Corddry. For half a century, give or take a year, Charlie Corddry has been covering the nation's defense establishment—first for United Press International and, since 1967, following in the distinguished tradition of Mark Watson, for the *Baltimore Sun*. He also, you will all recall, has been a regular on that lifeline for all of us, the *Washington Week in Review*. He is the Dean of the Pentagon reporters and, as befits a Dean, has been awarded, among his many awards, several honorary degrees. It's a pleasure to have Dr. Corddry with us today.

D is for Bob Donovan on my left. During the Eisenhower Administration, Bob was the White House Correspondent for the *New York Herald Tribune*, which was Ike's favorite newspaper. He later became the bureau chief and, subsequently, the bureau chief for the *Los Angeles Times*. During the Eisenhower Administration, he wrote the best seller "Eisenhower, the Inside

Story," and the story of how he wrote that story is very intriguing—I'm going to force him to tell it to us later today. He has truly been a student of presidents; his two-volume work of Harry Truman is a classic in the field of presidential biographies, and his book on John Kennedy's wartime exploits, "PT 109," you will recall is a major movie. For you Eisenhower fans, I also recommend a recent book called "Confidential Secretary," which concerns Ann Whitman's twenty years with Eisenhower and Rockefeller.

Tom Griscom at G on my right. Tom is now Thomas C. Griscom because he is now executive vice president of a great conglomerate, the R. J. Reynolds Co. When I first knew him in 1984, he was just "Tommy" and, at that time he was Howard Baker's press secretary in the United States Senate. Without a doubt, he was considered the best press secretary in the Senate, and there were some veteran reporters there who had even claimed that he was the best press secretary who has ever been on Capitol Hill. When Howard Baker went to the White House as Chief of Staff, Tom joined the President as the Director of Communications. Before coming to Washington, Tom was a reporter in Tennessee. So he has the unique qualifications of having served not only as a journalist but also in the executive and the legislature.

When we get to R, we get to Andy Rooney. I don't think anybody has probably called you Andrew, at least to my knowledge, except maybe your mother. He is our Andy Rooney. His unique reports, "A Few Minutes with Andy Rooney," have been a regular feature of "60 Minutes," with the exception of a few weeks this year. He wins Emmys the way the rest of us get parking tickets. And he is also an essayist whose weekly newspaper column appears in 250 newspapers. Oh, I should say that his connection with Ike is perhaps the longest of all of ours, in the sense that it goes back to World War II, when he was a young correspondent in the European Theater for *The Stars and Stripes*.

We now get to Ray Scherer. He started covering the White House for NBC when Harry Truman was President. He became chief correspondent when President Eisenhower took office and stayed with the Presidency throughout the administrations of

John Kennedy and Lyndon Johnson. He was the first radio correspondent to do a daily program from the White House. He was the only radio-TV reporter to be in Denver when President Eisenhower had his heart attack in 1955. I think that's a very important part of history in the relations of the media and the presidency and I'm going to ask Ray to talk about that later. He was with President Eisenhower so many times in Gettysburg, and I found out as he drove me around yesterday, that he could be a tour guide of the battlefield here. Maybe he will give us all a guided tour at some point.

We now come to Dan Schorr, who has literally done everything that a journalist can do: including being on a president's enemy list and almost being indicted by Congress once for not releasing his sources. He was first a newspaper reporter writing for the *New York Times* and the *Christian Science Monitor*. He then was a foreign correspondent in the Moscow bureau for CBS in 1955; he was even arrested there on trumped up charges—you can't seem to stay out of trouble, Dan. He was later the Bonn bureau chief. He returned to Washington as a correspondent where he's covered all the hearings that have a hyphen in them, such as Army-McCarthy, Iran-Contra, and so forth. He is a syndicated columnist who has written many books, the most recently co-authored with his wife. He is now the senior news analyst for the National Public Radio.

Let me explain the flight plan that we're going to be following during this morning's plenary session. We're going to divide our discussion into three unequal parts. I know that this is a symposium, a very serious word, but it is also a birthday party, and we want to celebrate that a bit too. So first, I'm going to ask our panelists to tell briefly, if they wish, their favorite Eisenhower story in the "Happy Birthday" tradition. And second, we're going to turn to the history of "The Media and Eisenhower"—discussing what happened during those years, how it was precedent-setting, what Eisenhower and the media's relations were. The primary people who will lead the discussion are those who were actually there in Washington at the time, and clearly everybody is encouraged to join in. Then we're going to conclude with the analysis: Presidents and the Press. Past and Present. Moving backward and forward. Here you have a panel, very humble, modest people and I'm going to encourage them to pretend that their book title is "Presidents Who Have Known Me," and they can tell us about that topic. Well, let's start with favorite stories. Tom Griscom, since you're the only person who doesn't have grey hair on the panel, do you still have a favorite?

Thomas Griscom: I was going to say, the only person who still has hair, but everybody else around here does too. Well Steve, let me tell you that what I want to do in this first part is to learn, like the people in the audience because I feel that this is a history lesson, a birthday party, and I'll be very frank—I was five years old when President Eisenhower took office. At five years old, I was not reading the *New York Times* or the *Washington Post* every day or glued in front of NBC television, so I'm going to sit back with you and learn from the other people we have up here with us.

Stephen Hess: Then let's do it chronologically. Probably, the first one with an experience with General Eisenhower would be the young *Stars and Stripes* reporter, Andy Rooney. Tell us what you remember.

Andy Rooney: Those introductory remarks of yours were very gracefully done, by the way. I have heard a lot of people do this and none as well as you just did that.

Stephen Hess: From Andy Rooney! Take note!

Andy Rooney: I started to write some notes and found I had so little to put down that I gave it up. So I didn't bring any notes with me to speak of. Eisenhower's Headquarters was at 20 Grosvenor Square in London when I was a reporter with the *Stars and Stripes.* We printed the papers in the austere offices of *The Times* of London. I went to my first press conference that General Eisenhower was holding. There was a group of people around a big, long table. I was 23, I guess, and plenty nervous. I was making notes as fast as I could, notes which I later couldn't read, a tradition in the business as I learned later. I had no idea how a press conference went. So after the thing was over, I took my notes and started to write my story. I did what I could with it, and the next day I read the report by Gladwyn Hill of the Associated Press, later of the *New York Times.* I was so young, it had never occurred to me that you didn't take what he said in the order of which he said it. I remember being shocked that Gladwyn Hill had lifted one of the last things that Eisenhower said and that was the headline of the story. That was a journalism lesson for me, I'll tell you! I would think that was enough from me.

I have one Eisenhower story that is tangential, I suppose. We had a great reporter named Bud Hutton, a sergeant. Eisenhower was such a protector of the press. He was just wonderful to us. I mean, the Army should have such a man now to protect us from their public relations people. This is what Bud Hutton did. One of the rules the censors had was, if it had been previously printed, you could write the story about it. So, Bud collected all these stories from all over the United States about the P-47, and we had not yet said that it was in England. It was a big secret and I was sent out to do the story and hold for release. The next day Bud put together his massive 8,000 word story on the P-47 and had all of the items that he had collected, showed them to the censor and the censor said, "Well, they have been printed before and, if they have been printed, you can use them." Although it was a great collection, it was a monumental job he had done. So the next day he wrote the story and General Hunter of the Air Force demanded Hutton's court-martial. The papers for Hutton's court-martial came into the desk, like a city desk in a newspaper, and Sgt. Hutton handled everything there and he just looked at these court-martial papers, wrote "Disapproved" on it and sent it back. It was months before it came up again and Hunter finally pressed it and it got to Eisenhower and Eisenhower was the one that finally salvaged Bud Hutton, our city editor, from court martial.

Stephen Hess: That's grand! Charlie Corddry, you too are probably going to be someone who wants to remember General Eisenhower, as opposed to President Eisenhower, so I'll ask you to go next.

Charles Corddry: Thank you. I think that there are great differences between General and President Eisenhower and doubtless, we'll get into them. But let me just tell you that, like Tommy Griscom, I'm here to listen to you old folks. When General Eisenhower came home from Europe he had a tumultuous welcome in Washington. He held a press conference at the

Pentagon and I was allowed to go. I'm not sure I was allowed to write it up, but I was allowed to go, because I might learn, Andy, where the lead was. In the course of this press conference, someone, I think it was Eddie Folliard, of the *Washington Post*, asked General Eisenhower if he had been worried when the Germans counter-attacked in the Ardennes, what became the Battle of the Bulge. Eisenhower was sometimes, not as President but as General, addicted to short answers and he said, "You bet! When I saw the papers from home!"

Stephen Hess: Well, sir, I think we should come to Martin Agronsky, because I know that he was president of the Congressional Radio and TV correspondents and early in the administration was invited to a rather intimate dinner at the White House, of which he was an interesting participant. Martin, do you want to chat?

Martin Agronsky: Yes, that was in 1954. I was president of the Congressional radio and TV galleries. What went with the job was an invitation to a White House dinner. That was one of the really important "perks" of the job. I was invited to my stag dinner at the White House at the height of the whole McCarthy business. At the time, he was going after the Secretary of the Army Stevens, and he and that dreadful Roy Cohn and that horrible David Schine were going after the national press corps, *(turning to Ray Scherer)* you remember that?...

Ray Scherer: Yes.

Martin Agronsky: It was a difficult time for reporters. In any case, there were a lot of rich people eating dinner there. Actually, the chief man there was Hunt from Texas and he had flown in quail for the White House dinner, it wasn't bad. At each place, and I thought that this was vulgar and cheap and wrong, there was a little white plastic figure of Eisenhower with his hands raised. Do you remember that he'd raise his hands for people to stop applauding. I saved it, of course; but I really didn't like it and I thought, "Ike doesn't need this and why the hell does he do something like that?" The dinner went on and I must say that it was not a very comfortable dinner for a reporter. They were talking about McCarthy calling reporters communists which, you remember was a very usual gimmick of McCarthy. They also talked about how dreadful reporters were and how they were going after this magnificent patriarch. Then Hunt began to say that everyone knew that reporters were communists. As a reporter at the White House with the President of the United States, I was very reluctant to speak up. *(Turning to Ray Scherer)* You and I had a situation like that, you remember with Lyndon Johnson?

Ray Scherer: Yes, another dinner.

Martin Agronsky: Another dinner. Anyway, this went on with these people making absolutely dreadful statements about how we were communists and liars, whatever we did. Nobody, of course, came to the defense of the reporter. I thought, "This is intolerable and I shouldn't do it but I'm going to answer," which I did. I merely said something like, "Mr. Hunt, I think you are mistaken when you equate criticism with disloyalty or treason. Reporters are good Americans like other Americans, and it's a great mistake to denounce us as traitors. If you're looking for treason and traitors and people who are doing damage to our country, you can look on Capitol Hill, and there sits Senator McCarthy who is, I think, doing an enormous amount of damage to our country." Now Ike never said a word during this exchange, he just sort of nodded, but that proved to quiet them down a bit. They were annoyed with me, I'm sure, but you know, I didn't give a damn. The dinner went on, we finished and, to my amazement, when the dinner was over and we were going to the door, Ike walked around the table. He came and put his arm around my shoulders and walked me to the door! I was very nervous but I didn't know what to say to him. He turned and said to me as we were walking along, "I'm glad that you answered Mr. Hunt." And I still didn't know what to say to him, I said, "Well, you know, I felt that it had to be said." And he said, "It did have to be said and you were right." He walked me out the door and that was the end of it. I always felt as a reporter that nobody ever really got close to Eisenhower. I didn't know him well. I don't think any of us really knew him well. I don't think that he meant it that way, but he was withdrawn, very reserved, very much the General of the Army and the President of the United States. At least I always felt that in my dealings with him.

Stephen Hess: Well, let's hold that part of your discussion,

Martin, for the part about Eisenhower and the Media and continue quickly with the favorite stories.

Bob Donovan, you were there the longest, can you sort one out of your store?

Robert Donovan: Apropos, last night's session dwelled for some time on whether President Eisenhower could be angry but wrathful, I think, was really the meaning. One of my favorite stories of Ike bears upon that point. We were in Denver with him for two and half months in the summer of 1954. He stayed and worked in Denver, but then on weekends he would go up and fish with a friend of his in the mountains. Before going to fish on a Sunday morning, he had attended a prayer breakfast in Denver and he delivered one of his favorite speeches on spiritual values— he called them spiritual values. Most of us wrote stories about Eisenhower's talk and then we went to the mountains to watch the fishing. There was Ike, hauling them in and so forth, and we all wrote a small story about that. The next morning, *The New York Times* arrived on President Eisenhower's desk at the Air Base there and there was an explosion! At the bottom of *The New York Times,* the editors had put those two stories side by side on the front page and the headline read "Eisenhower Extols Spiritual Values—Over Catches Legal Limit of Fish." The reason I know that Eisenhower was ruffled by it was that Hagerty opened the door like a drunken sailor in the pressroom and delivered an obscene speech to us. He said, "You know what you guys are gonna get from now on?" Well, I won't answer it. But that was approximately the headline.

Stephen Hess: Dan, let's have a good Eisenhower story.

Daniel Schorr: Well, you asked earlier for a favorite story and I have one—my wife says I cannot tell it at a birthday celebration but I may tell it later. I will tell you this one now.

Early in the Eisenhower administration in 1953, the staff was still new and didn't know the President's habits or friends. One day the President went to his secretary and said, "Get me George Allen. Tell him to come up here about 6:00 o'clock to the family entrance," and left. The secretary had never heard of George Allen and made a lot of discreet inquiries, found out that there was a George V. Allen, the Ambassador to Yugoslavia, who had just arrived in Washington for consultations. She called the State Department. Allen was told the President, whom he had never met, wanted to see him, and to go up to the family entrance. He went there at 6:00 o'clock, President Eisenhower looked down the stairs and saw him and said, "Hello." He said, "Mr. President, I'm George Allen, you sent for me." He said, "Are you George Allen, the friend of Presidents?" He said, "I'm Ambassador to Yugoslavia, sir." Eisenhower asked him to come upstairs, asked how he was doing, got a briefing on Yugoslavia, thanked him for having dropped in and Allen left. Three days later, the Secretary of State, John Foster Dulles, called on the President in the Oval Office to discuss ambassadorial appointments. He said, "We have Paris, we have Rome, we have London, I don't yet have a recommendation to make for you on India." The President said, "Really? How about this George Allen? He seems to be a pretty nice chap." And George V. Allen became ambassador to India.

Thomas Griscom: That was repeated in the 80's. This is history. I think I've witnessed some of those same experiences during my time in the White House.

Stephen Hess: Ray, tell us your story.

Ray Scherer: Well, Eisenhower held a news conference every Wednesday morning from 10:30 to 11:00, and these were very big events; sometimes they were front page stories in the *Times* the next morning. Walter Lippmann would come. Scotty Reston would come. Eric Severaid. Izzy Stone. Everybody came because it wasn't on television. It wasn't on radio and the only way you could see Eisenhower up close was to come to these conferences. He would cover maybe 15 to 20 subjects in 30 minutes. My job was to go on the air at 11:00 o'clock and give a coherent account of what he had said. This was sometimes difficult because Eisenhower has this wandering syntax which is, I guess, the point of my story, which I'll get to in a moment; you didn't always know what he really meant. At any rate, at 11 o'clock, Merriman Smith would say, "Thank you, Mr. President," and we'd run out of the room. I'd go right into the phone booth and Frank Blair, who was doing the news from New York radio, would say, "President Eisenhower has just finished a news conference and here is Ray Scherer with what he said;" then I would blurt forth a minute and a half of highlights. The office in New York would keep score to see how it checked out with what AP said was the lead and what UPI said was the lead and more often than not, we agreed. In retrospect, I don't know quite how I did this; it was a trick that I had mastered. Well, I found out later in Eisenhower's memoirs, that when he obfuscated or lead us down the garden path, it was deliberate. There was the case of Quemoy and Matsu. The question was: Would Eisenhower use force in case the Chinese communists came over against the Nationalists? The State Department went to Hagerty and said the President must not answer this, it's a very delicate subject. If he says he's going to use "the bomb," it would upset the whole world as happened in Truman's case. If he says he's not going to use it, that opens things up for the Chinese communists. So at any rate, before the news conference, Hagerty said to Eisenhower, "Mr. President, this is a very tricky one and you're going to have to handle this with great care. If you say this, you'll have this problem and if you say that, you'll have this problem." He looked at Hagerty and he said, "Don't worry, Jim, I'll just confuse them." So, if we sounded confused in our reporting on what the President said, it was all very deliberate. He used ambiguity and he was very good at it.

Stephen Hess: Thank you. I have a very little story. I kept a diary during those two and a half years. I was looking through it the other day for a little story and this one is dated Oct. 13, 1959. At 9:00 a.m., we presented the President two gifts for his 69th birthday. A huge cake and a red maple tree for the White House lawn. Hurrying to the presentation ceremony, Fay Steiner, who was one of the secretaries, unexpectedly ran into the President. "I'm late," she stammered. "Well," he said, "it's all right, they can't do anything until we arrive." He could be a very charming man when he wanted to be.

Let's turn now to the question of Ike and the Media. I thought maybe we would start the discussions with the questions being touched on in his news conferences. He held 193 of them in eight years and, if you'll recall at the time, what we most noted was the fractured syntax. I think now perhaps it's time for a re-evaluation. Dan Schorr told me that he spent a bit of the summer (that's the conscientious guy that he is) re-reading Eisenhower press conferences, including questions asked by Bob

Donovan and Ray Scherer. *(Turning to Dan Schorr)* Start us off on this, you have most recently read the transcripts.

Dan Schorr: Yes, Steve. Well, in the first place, it was remarkable to go back to them and look back on the time when the President seemed to hold news conferences virtually every week, uninterruptedly; apparently not afraid to face the press as some of his recent successors were. As I recall, and refresh my memory, he started out in early 1953 a little bit nervously. He gave himself an introduction; said he's always gotten along with the press; he'd like to get along with the press, would hope to be able to tell them as much as he could tell them, although there were some things he couldn't tell them about—they would have to forgive him; and then sort of laid down ground rules, explaining that if they wanted more, there was Jim Hagerty in the Press Office.

I thought that his press conferences developed a certain pattern. There were some matters that he didn't know very much about. There was one black reporter, Payne, who I think is still there, who almost every week would ask a question keyed to the subject of civil rights, minorities or problems of the poor. Most of the times the President would say such things as, "Yes, well, I have to look that one up," or turn to Jim Hagerty and say, "Make a note of that." He was very candid in indicating areas that he didn't know much about. His obfuscation was saved for more important questions than merely revealing his ignorance. There were a whole series of questions he just put aside; he said he didn't know the answer. There were other questions about matters that didn't seem to interest him much and he gave some pro forma answers. There were occasions, however, about such matters as war and peace or important principles that concerned him—nuclear energy, getting along with the Russians, getting along with NATO, coalition building, how it is that you get along with other countries when they don't agree, how you must bring them along with you instead of trying to bludgeon them. On such matters, he would sometimes go off on an almost eloquent statement of the things that he really believed; then he was at his best. It was usually at that time that Ray, Bob or somebody would say, "Can we quote that?" You see, in those early days of 1953, 1954, 1955, these things were still considered to be background and not available for quotation and God, certainly not available for radio and television and *never live*. In order to preserve some of his words, it became necessary to ask special permission. He would somewhat modestly say, "Well, let me get Jim to work on the syntax and clear up my grammar and maybe we'll let you use that." We have a series of great statements of the President which we forget although we are so much more accustomed to remember the one which maybe was intentionally confusing to us. I suggest on some occasions he was *not* intentionally confusing us at all but simply going off into a meandering kind of "stream-of-consciousness" way of speaking that sometimes left some of the people frustrated. He "reads" a lot better today than he sounded to us then.

Stephen Hess: Ray, you covered four presidents and their press conferences. Did the Eisenhower years have a special resonance, a special importance, in the history of this institution?

Ray Scherer: Eisenhower did a lot to institutionalize the presidential news conference. In Roosevelt's day, it was reporters standing around the desk and it was all in the third person...the President said this, the President said that...you couldn't quote him directly. In the Truman years, it was the same thing. Occasionally, you could get something particularly succinct after Truman said it and they would ask special permission and you could do it first person. Almost from the beginning, we were allowed to tape record Eisenhower's news conferences. Hagerty would clear them for us; he kept the franchise on whether or not to release the whole news conference. Invariably, he would say, "Go ahead, take it all." This gave Eisenhower a new hold on public opinion in the sense that his news conferences were reported on radio every Wednesday; then 1955 came along and they decided it was time to take the news conference in to the television era. Eisenhower had been brought along, carefully, by Hagerty and decided this would give him another dimension. Hagerty called us in and said could we put cameras in there without blinding the President? Yes, we could. At the time, there was a new film out, 400 speed, that didn't need many lights. Could you go for a whole half hour without changing film magazines and having a lot of clatter in the back of the room? Yes, we could. Well, these were technical things, but they made it possible for Eisenhower to go on television. So that meant that every Wednesday night from then on, on the Douglas Edwards news and the Swayze news, there was Eisenhower speaking to the people. He did not go live. We used to ask Hagerty about that and his response was, "Well, he might misspeak himself." Well, he never did but it did give the news conference a new dimension. Jack Kennedy took the next step by going live. But it brought Eisenhower into every home.

Stephen Hess: We're starting to get a picture of Eisenhower with a staff that was much more savvy about public opinion and it's uses than perhaps we thought. That may be the introduction to you, Bob, on this remarkable story about how you happened to write "Eisenhower, the Inside Story."

Robert Donovan: Television, needless to say, is really an enormous force in America today. We see it all over the place and it really came into existence, as far as the White House was concerned, in the Eisenhower administration. Television I think, is one of the real landmarks of the Eisenhower presidency. There was no television when Truman was in office, none to speak of. Here is some background on this. After Dewey was defeated by Truman in 1948, he eventually decided to run again for governor in 1950. At this time, the television industry was centered in New York and advertising agencies were based in New York. Dewey was very close to the television and advertising industry. He began to develop techniques that have been used ever since. I believe it was Dewey who had the first call-in talk show on television. Hagerty was Dewey's press secretary during this period and Hagerty became interested in television and advertising and the possible uses for these mediums in politics. Eisenhower was president of Columbia University in those years. Dewey, Hagerty and Eisenhower were often in New York at the same time learning about the potentiality of television. This meant that, when Eisenhower decided to run for President, he was ahead of the field in the use of television. Hagerty was the pioneer of how to use television and of how to relate the White House to television (I think that is one of Hagerty's most important points). Eisenhower had been running against Taft when his nomination was contested on what was then called a moral issue. Taft was trying to have certain Eisenhower delegates not seated at the convention. Eisenhower seized upon this moral issue and delivered television speeches that, even before the convention, were very effective. So, I think that, when you talk about Eisenhower and the media and his relationship with people, you have to see him as sort of a pioneer in the use of what has commonly become an enormous force in the world.

Ray Scherer: Let me interrupt if I may. He was the first presidential candidate to be featured in a thirty second commercial, actually, they were twenty seconds. *Eisenhower Answers America.* His media people got together and they sorted out the three issues that were most important: one was peace, one was Korea, and one was, I think, inflation. They concocted twenty-one commercials in which Ike gave the answer; found people to ask the questions and spliced them together. They were a very big part of the campaign.

Stephen Hess: The commercial break, at this point, is that Scherer and Bob Donovan, who are now senior fellows, or some title like that, at the Wilson Center in Washington, are co-authoring a book on the impact of the first 40 years of TV news.

Charlie Corddry, I want to ask you this. Eisenhower had a fascinating buffer system, as you know. He was eight years in the Presidency, we had a lot of trouble with agriculture at that time but everybody always blamed Ezra Taft Benson, never the President. In fact, Jim Hagerty tells the classic story about how the President would call Jim in and say, "I want you to do it this way," and Jim would say, "Mr. President, if I go out there and do it that way at my next meeting with the press, they are going to give me hell." Ike got up, walked around the desk and patted Jim on the back and said, "My boy, better you than me."

(To Charles Corddry:) Now you lived through all of this, three Secretaries of Defense and a President who was a five-star general. What can one say about how the media and the administration operated?

Charles Corddry: Well, I think that he could off load blame very adroitly. It has to be said right off that Eisenhower was indeed his own Secretary of Defense. Charles Wilson, the former President of General Motors, held the title, and I must say endeared himself to those of us who covered him because he was so outspoken. But, I think Eisenhower was the fellow who decided what he was going to do; and what he was going to do was not to the liking of the people who have a tendency toward believing in huge military power—a very strange thing for a five-star general—but he came off as anti-military from time to time. I would like to say this about Secretary of Defense Wilson and the first press conference he ever had. We were still following the White House rules; some comments were on the record, some were not, and some were for indirect attribution. We'd say, "Can we quote you?" and he would say, "You can quote me on everything." He never, ever was off the record or on background and he always told it the way he saw it.

The way that the story was supposed to go is that we would not let anything like money interfere with building the defenses we needed; so, we're not going to cut just to save money. I remember one night they had a meeting at the White House. Wilson came back to the Pentagon, I forget what year this is—well into the administration—and economics were a bit dicey. Wilson came back to the Pentagon and said we're going to cut "x" thousand men out of service, we're going to cut "x" billion dollars. We said, "We thought you didn't let financial issues interfere with the mounting of defense." He said, "Well, I'm going to this time." Ike had told him exactly what he was going to do and he came back and did it. I don't know whether that's responsive or not.

Stephen Hess: Okay, before we slip into our third part, I do want Ray Scherer to get "on the record" the story about the Eisenhower heart attack in '55, because this was, I think we would all agree, a turning point in how the presidency dealt with health issues. That, of course, became very important, particularly in the last administration.

Ray Scherer: Well, Ike was aware that in Woodrow Wilson's time, his illness was kept from the people and Mrs. Wilson took over. Poor Joe Tumulty, who was press secretary, was completely out of things, lost his prestige and practically disappeared from the scene. President Eisenhower was also disturbed by what happened in Harding's time; his illness was clouded over; even in FDR's time, when, in his last year, Ross McIntyre and others kept from the public the fact that Roosevelt was really a dying man. You could see it in his face but the people didn't really know it.

In September of 1955, we were again out in Denver. Eisenhower had just come back from fishing at Frazier and Ann Whitman remarked that he never looked better. He played golf that day, had a hamburger with sliced onion for lunch and had a little indigestion. He was bedeviled on the golf course by phone calls from Foster Dulles; he'd go all the way back to the clubhouse and somehow, the phone didn't work and I think it got his dander up. It may have caused what happened that night. He woke up at 2:30 a.m. with a pain in his chest. Dr. Snyder was brought in. He thought it was a heart attack. He brought in electrocardiograms the next day, Saturday, and they determined it was a heart attack. They walked back down the narrow steps of Mrs. Doud's home, put him in a car and took him to the hospital. Then Murray Snyder (it's a long story with a lot of details) called us out to Lowry Field and said the President had just suffered an attack of coronary thrombosis. We all raced to the phones and put it on the air. I happened to be the only reporter there at the time working for radio and television. CBS was not covering. ABC wasn't covering either—to their eternal regret. At any rate, the question then was how to handle this thing. Jim Hagerty was on vacation; he flew back and talked to Dr. Snyder. Dr. Snyder said that the President said, "Let Jim handle it." Ike apparently had a momentary conversation with Jim in which he said, "Come clean." And from then on, they made public every detail of Eisenhower's heart attack, every detail of his recovery, what his temperature was, what his heart beat was, what he ate, what music he listened to, and who visited him. It even got to the point, when Dr. Paul Dudley White told us he had had a rather successful bowel movement, we put that on the air. It bothered some of our listeners, but it was part of the recovery process. I guess the point is that they set a new standard in telling everything. This brought credibility and it buttressed Eisenhower's case for running again when he finally made the decision to run again. He had credibility, people believed him, they thought they'd heard the whole story and I think they had. He had many other illnesses: he had ileitis, he had a small stroke and, in each case, Hagerty told all.

Stephen Hess: *(Turning to Robert Donovan)*. Go ahead. Last comment before we go into the Presidency and the Press.

Robert Donovan: Dan has raised the question of Eisenhower using deliberate obfuscation in his press conference and I know he did that. I, myself, am skeptical about how much this was used, but the point I want to make is this: all during those years the biggest joke in the country was Eisenhower's syntax and the way Eisenhower answered questions at press conferences. All sorts of jokes were built around it. I attended every press conference President Eisenhower ever held and I never knew a reporter who did not understand what Eisenhower was saying. Furthermore, when Kennedy of Harvard, a polished candidate, from the London School of Economics, a dapper man, got on the stage and began holding his press conferences, *Time* magazine suddenly had the idea of taking an excerpt from Eisenhower's press conference and an excerpt from Kennedy's press conference and ran them together. When Kennedy read them, he had a fit.

Stephen Hess: Dan.

Daniel Schorr: I'm obliged to tell the story now that my wife does not want me to. It really wasn't always true; we generally had a fair idea of what President Eisenhower was trying to say. Sometimes it came through wrong. Sometimes he said things that he didn't really want to say and which actually opposed the known policy of the government. I remember one occasion, when I walked out of the press conference in that old Indian Treaty Room in the Executive Office Building. I walked out with James "Scotty" Reston. We were discussing something the President had said which had to be wrong. And I said to Scotty, "How do you think Jim Hagerty will explain this one this afternoon?" Because in the afternoon, there were these explanations as to what the President really meant. I said, "How do you think this will be explained by Jim Hagerty?" Scotty stopped for a minute, he said, "I think that Jim, this time, will have to say that 'President Eisenhower does not necessarily speak for this administration.'"

Stephen Hess: All right. There will be no rebuttal. Let's open this up. I brought something to ask Tommy Griscom. What in heavens name is happening in these thirty (30) years. This is from something that was done at the Harvard-Joan Shorenstein Barone Center on the Press, Politics and Public Policy where they compared the 1968 presidential campaign to the 1988 presidential campaign. But I think this applies. The author said, "The average sound bite, or block, of uninterrupted speech fell from 42.3 seconds for presidential candidates in 1968 to only 9.8 seconds in 1988. In 1968, almost half of all sound bites were 40 seconds or more compared to less than 1% in 1988. In fact, it was not uncommon in 1968, for a candidate to speak uninterrupted for over a minute on the evening news. That was 21% of the sound bite. In 1988, it never happened." Tom, what's going on? Is this indicative of something that has brought us from some substantial view of the President to manipulated snippets?

Thomas Griscom: Well, I think part of it is the impact of television. I will tell you I had been a print reporter before I went to Washington. In Washington, you understand quickly that television reaches not just the American people, but the whole world instantaneously. When we went to the White House after spending six years in the Senate with the Majority Leader, we did not fully appreciate the fact that, when the President speaks or when a key staff person speaks, it is out immediately and everywhere; because you have one news source, unlike 535 who serve on Capitol Hill. Part of it though, Steve, is trying to understand TV. Television is not just news; it's also the correspondent who reports the news. The correspondents become important people. There are certain traits that people attribute to that reporter so they become an integral part of the story. Therefore, reporters are competing for 23 minutes of news which is going across this country and they have got to get a piece on the air. You, as a news source, have to learn how to talk and keep it from being edited. That's what you're trying to do.

I'll give you a quick example. When we were dealing with Iran-Contra, President Reagan went on the road. We drove through Wisconsin; almost a whistle stop campaign in cars. We decided that one of the things we needed to say was that Reagan was going to be active; he was not going to be caught up in the White House, leaving the impression similar to what happened during Watergate, that the President was trapped and could not function. So we built a line in the speech where the President of the United States said, "I am not a potted plant." There were some people saying, "This is not Presidential" and we said, "Hey, we don't really care, it will get covered." President Reagan said it three times and sure enough, the lead story was that President Reagan today went out and told the American people, "I'm not a potted plant." What we're trying to get across is the fact that, "I am not going to be sitting here planted in this office; I am going to do something." But I think you have to try to understand the medium that you're working with and how to deal with it. I do think there is a function the White House has to perform in getting its side of the news out; then letting a reporter work on it and figure out how to present it. The sound bite is very much there.

Stephen Hess: Andy, you are still heavily engaged in the television media. How does it look to you?

Andy Rooney: Well, the fact of the matter is that no one writes as he speaks or speaks as he writes. The problem for anyone who writes well for television is to make a compromise between the two styles. I think that more politicians have learned to make that compromise between the writing style and the speaking style, finding some middle ground. That's why the takes have gotten shorter, they have just learned how to do it better.

Ray Scherer: They know what will get on the air. They plot them in advance and put them out there and sure enough they are picked up.

Stephen Hess: But what about a medium in which the anchors now seem to be more celebrities than the President of the United States? Isn't there something that has changed the balance?

Andy Rooney: Now, let's keep this on a high level, Steve.

Stephen Hess: Oh, absolutely, absolutely. Strike that from the record. Martin.

Martin Agronsky: That's another field. We can talk about that the rest of the day and it does not interest me particularly. I think that we are forgetting, with Hagerty for example, or Pierre Salinger, Kennedy's liaison, that you're dealing with guys who studied the media people and who wanted to use it and wanted to use it most effectively for their good. It was no accident that you had quotable statements, pieces of little bites from Kennedy, for example; or that Ike's stuff was constantly being condensed and contracted. Hagerty would say to him when they talked about something, "If you would say this, Mr. President, this way, that would be very effective." That was happening all the time, Ray, and it should have happened because these guys were professionals, they were trying to get the most out of their people and that's what they were doing. Whether we were aware of it or not, and most of us were, that's what was happening.

Stephen Hess: Ray, do you want to jump in and tell the audience. Come on.

Ray Scherer: This may be premature, maybe something you may want to get in to later, but the relationship between reporters and the president is completely changed since the days of Mr. Eisenhower. Sam Donaldson wouldn't have lasted five minutes with Mr. Eisenhower. He was an ex-general, he was the President, we held him in a certain awe and you just wouldn't pop questions at him the way that Sam has done. But the environment wasn't there.

Thomas Griscom: What you run into though, is that you sit there and say, "Okay, let's deal with that type of reporter." This means, somebody says, "Well you're out of business," to quote a famous line that another press secretary used. Everybody says you can't do it because all of the sudden, if you're not seen on television for an extended period of time, then people think that the President's not doing something, anything; so to me, Ray, one of the changes that happened is that, with the power of television, you have to look at that trade off. Can you afford to say I'm going to ignore this person and then all of a sudden, you get a black out on television? This really does impair your ability to govern because television, whether we like it or not, is the way that we quite often govern in this country today. That's how people understand what's going on in government today. They make that assessment very quickly from what they hear every night. What was important today? What did the President say? What did he not say?

Stephen Hess: Do you want to bring the print media back into this?

Charles Corddry: Yes. A question comes to mind—I don't have the answer to it—of whether the presidential press conference nowadays is giving us information as much as it used to or less than it used to. Are presidents using it for straightforward communication of information to the public? I remember being in the Oval Office, I don't know whether you were there or not, when Truman said, "Hitler is Dead." We went back the next week and said, "How do you know that," and he said, "Well, Himmler said so and if anybody knew, he would." But when Eisenhower (we've talked about whether he could speak English) was having a bit of trouble with Khrushchev, we thought that they were going to roll over Berlin. He said at a press conference, "We are certainly not going to fight a ground war in Europe." Now, you have to take yourself back to the late 1950's to figure out what he really was telling the world. Peter Lisagor, who is revered still by all of us, I am sure, asked him, "Well, then, what *ARE* you going to do because you don't like nuclear weapons?" And the President said, "I didn't say that nuclear war is a complete impossibility." Well, this really stirred up the Europeans and got things settled down on the other side of the Iron Curtain, as I remember. Dan may have a different recollection. I don't know whether press conferences are used nowadays to respond to the people's legitimate questions; and I mean you students here...

Stephen Hess: But, more has happened, certainly, in those years in a relationship between the present government, the press and the presidency. Tell us, what about Vietnam? What about Watergate? What's going on? Isn't there a different relationship, a part of which the government has brought on?

Daniel Schorr: There are several relationships. The relationship of television with the White House is necessarily a relationship of subservience because you need those pictures. You need the access and no matter how, no matter what snide remark you may make at the end of the piece, you are basically transmitting the message that the public relations person, or Michael Deaver, the executive producer in the White House, wants to have transmitted. We can pretend that we're all being very tough. For toughness, for analysis, we really have to depend more on the print media than on television. Television is a theater, you know. All the White House is a stage and all the rest of us are merely players. Even President Nixon at times learned the way in which he could use the press as a buffer against himself—he could play against them. President Reagan played against them. President Reagan constantly looked like the victim of these people. President Bush is *not* quite so adept at it but he's having other troubles. And so on. But let us face the fact that when you transfer journalists into a medium of theater, the dominant theme of it from then on becomes theater and whoever knows how to exploit theater wins.

Andy Rooney: Steve, I just have the feeling that every president we have ever had exposed to television feels that he has been done wrong by the media and, specifically, by television; yet I feel that for all the bad things that we do with television, for all they are able to manipulate television, the American public ends up knowing a president better than that president knows himself and it's *because* of television.

Stephen Hess: Okay, Tom and then Martin.

Thomas Griscom: I just want to pick up on what Dan talked about, the fact that having a picture is very important. We understood that when we were brought in to deal with Iran-Contra. We made a decision that, when the hearings were going on up on the Hill, the story ought to stay up there. Now, we had a lot of White House correspondents who were upset. They were trying to get the president out to say something because that would then bring the story back to the White House. They could then link it back; but we were aware of the fact that we did not need to have that story rolling back into the White House every night. Congress was dealing with it and we wanted it up there. Also, we were trying to build on the fact that the President was not covered by the Boland Amendment. I wanted to add some of those things to your point. We got a lot of heat from reporters because they knew that to get on the air they had to have the President of the United States saying something; but we sat there and figured out that, for us to be able to deal with the problem we had, we needed to keep that story on the Hill. I think your point is well made and we do understand and appreciate the way that stories are put together.

Stephen Hess: Martin, jump in.

Martin Agronsky: I would like to make a point. When we're talking about what we did get, what we didn't get was terribly important too. Let's go back to the period of the French and Dien Bien Phu when they were going under. The Vice President of the United States, Richard Nixon, *(having trouble with his microphone...some adjustment of the microphone follows.)*

I'll start from the beginning. We're concerned about talking about what we did get and I think we should also be concerned with what we didn't get. It was very interesting, the things we didn't get. That always struck me in the Eisenhower administration.

Looking toward the panel: You guys have all covered it, I wonder if you'd agree with me. I feel that one of the things that mattered most of all to us at that point was: would the United States be involved in coming to the aid of the French, you remember, at Dien Bien Phu. Nixon was totally committed to that. Douglas was totally committed to that. I think we would have been in it if not for Eisenhower, who rejected it. I remember three or four times raising that particular question in various ways at Ike's news conferences and he ducked them. He wasn't ready to talk about it. He certainly wasn't ready to talk about it publicly. The pressures came from Nixon; they came from Douglas; and Ike kind of walked away from it. I always thought it was a failure on our part that we were never able to get Eisenhower's position from him at that point. Later, we did get it but at that point we didn't need it. I think that we failed and we failed badly.

Stephen Hess: Bob, come in at this point because you were the only reporter I've ever known who was given a "Q" clearance by the Eisenhower or by any presidential administration. Do you want to add to what we know and how we know it?

Robert Donovan: As timely as I can. Wintergil Veere wrote in the *New Yorker* that this was quite possibly the boldest thing the Eisenhower administration ever did. In the spring of 1955, I was the White House correspondent for the *Herald Tribune*. I got a call from a member of the White House staff named Kevin McCann, whom reporters didn't deal with very much, and he asked me, in brief, "Could you and I have lunch somewhere where no other reporter would be likely to see us?" We worked that out. He said that the White House would like to have a book about the President written and, if a writer would do it, they would guarantee to give him any information he wanted. Well, we've all heard that stuff! I said no, I wouldn't do it, and besides obviously, this book was to come out in 1956, which was a political year and it would have the earmark of a political book, which I didn't even know how to write, and I turned him down on it. Some time passed and he came back to me again. We went through this whole thing and he began to tell me a little more about NSC papers and about minutes of the Cabinet and so on but I still said, "no." He and I were walking back. I was going back to the Press Building and he was going back to the White House. He said, "Well it's a shame you're turning this down because this material would be great material in the *Herald Tribune.*" Well, that really gave me pause—am I doing something that's hurting the paper here? So I said, "Can I rethink this?" He said, "Come and see Sherman Adams." I went to see Adams and he pretty much repeated the story. I said, "How can I read National Security Council papers?" and he said, "I will have to get you a 'Q' clearance." That was the highest security clearance in the government at that time except possibly the Atomic Energy field. I said, "Well, let me talk to my publisher," and I did. He was awfully interested. It was Brownie Reed then. So I agreed to do it. This was already around May of 1955. I promised that the book would be published in June of 1956, which was a terribly short span. I started researching but I had to wait on the "Q" clearance; it took a long time. I'm not going into the "Q" clearance because that's another story. But I was astounded by what the "Q" clearance turned up in my life. I just couldn't believe it. Furthermore, some of it was so ambiguous that these people might have said," Oh, oh, let's not get mixed up with this guy, we'll just get the President in trouble," and so forth.

Just briefly, I was…oh, it's too long a story.

Stephen Hess: But it's all going to be in your book.

Robert Donovan: No, no.

Stephen Hess: No, it's not going to be in your book.

Robert Donovan: But this business, these complaints about government investigation, there's some merit to them. I started out working. The President was in Denver, that was the summer he had the heart attack, but it hadn't occurred yet; and, while

I was going to write the book at home, I was going to do the research down there at the White House. I was given Robert Montgomery's office. Montgomery was the television coach to the President, a former movie actor. I had long lists of what material was available from the National Security Council, the Defense Department, and this and that and the other thing, and I checked these things off and gave them to the attendant and later the attendant would come back with a *wheelbarrow*, with a *wheelbarrow* full of *top secret documents*. I'd take these documents. There was at that time a big dispute with the British over the sale of generators. I won't get into all that, but it was taken as an important issue at the time and there were a lot of stories about it. I'd pick this stuff up, British generator, the President and the National Security Council, and say, "Oh, I haven't got time for this" and off it would go; then another subject would come along, "Top Secret," I'd read it and think, God, I would never get through all that.

I don't think that anyone knows the story, I don't believe they do. If Eisenhower saw me in there reading some of that stuff, people last night would have known whether he had a temper or not. I can't believe he knew. I was in his correspondence, and I could have embarrassed him terribly if I had used some of that correspondence. I made a self-imposed rule that I wouldn't take any of this material to embarrass him. I could have embarrassed Democrats, high ranking Democrats, who wrote Eisenhower telling him how to really get at the Democrats. These were very distinguished people.

I tried to work out a very severe ground rule with Governor Adams on this. One rule was, and I understood this, that anything I took from "Top Secret" documents would have to be reviewed. A writer would have to expect that and I agreed to it; but I was so rigid about that, that sometimes I would just cut out a section from some big document and paste it on a piece of paper to be cleared.

A big business then was the "New Look" in the military and I requested that information and I got the National Security Council documents on the New Look in the military. I read them and I thought I could be in journalism for a lifetime and I would never write anything as clear as these documents were written;

and so, I paraphrased those documents. Instead of writing them, I paraphrased them. I couldn't make them any clearer. Well, all the sudden, Andy Goodpaster called me and said, "You must come to a meeting in Sherman's office this afternoon." This was getting well on into the writing of the book and the deadline was a terrible problem for me. I walked in and there was Sherman and a Mr. Anderson who was from Texas. It wasn't the Secretary of the Treasury. He was head of the National Security Council, this man named Anderson. All right. He was in there with a memo from the National Security Council demanding that Sherman Adams cancel this book after *all* the *blood* that had been shed over it. And Sherman said, "Why," and the first thing he did was pick up my chapter on the New Look, and pick up the document, and said to Sherman Adams (and he wasn't shy of Sherman Adams), he said, "Anyone in intelligence can read this chapter and see where this came from and how authentic it is," and I said, "Well, Mr. Anderson, all right, I'll do that over again;" but that wasn't enough. He had a whole list of reasons why the White House should kill this book and I didn't disagree with all of them. This was an extraordinary thing to have come out at that time. Mind you, historians like Professor Ambrose and Fred Reed and others didn't get these papers for twenty years. Adams picked it up. Adams, Sherman Adams, was white-faced and shaking under this attack from Anderson; and I think Anderson had raised a number of points that Adams hadn't considered. He said, "I'll take this to the President." He picked the papers up and walked out. I said, "Oh, my God, it's all over," you know? I said, "Well, we'll probably have about half an hour here to wait for Sherman to come back but what's he going to come back with?" Then Sherman came back, walked to the chair, sat down and said, "The President approved this." I honestly don't believe that Sherman Adams ever went to the President. I honestly do not believe he did it—no one should *ever* underestimate the powers that Sherman Adams had at his prime.

There was a fellow named Cutler who was National Security Advisor to the President. He was so strict.

Let me tell you one thing. This book was Number One on *The New York Times* Best Seller List for three months.

Stephen Hess: Let's conclude this. Let me read, in conclusion, what Dwight Eisenhower said in his memoirs about his relations with the press. He said, "I was able to avoid causing the nation a serious setback through anything I said in many hours over eight years of intensive questioning. It is far better to stumble, or speak guardedly, than to move ahead smoothly and risk imperiling the country." I think he viewed continuous interaction with the press as necessary, as absolutely part of the job description of the Presidency; although for him, and for most presidents, it's not a very pleasant part of their responsibilities. Yet, as we think back, this was a uniquely healthy attitude and one could wish that all future presidents, post-Eisenhower presidents, had shared his view. Thank you very much for coming and on to the next panels.

CHAPTER THREE

The Eisenhower Legacy in Civil Rights

One of the most important accomplishments of the Eisenhower administration's eight years in office was their record on civil rights. Two major civil rights bills were passed under President Eisenhower's leadership and the President signed executive orders which desegregated the city of Washington, D.C., integrated the armed forces, and brought unprecedented numbers of blacks into the executive branch, including the White House staff. In addition, President Eisenhower established the Government Contracts Committee, which provided that every government contractor have a clause which prohibited discrimination on the basis of race or color.

To discuss this are the four key players in the administration who orchestrated the civil rights programs. They are Maxwell Rabb and Rocco Siciliano of the White House staff, Attorney General Herbert Brownell, and Secretary of Health, Education and Welfare Arthur Flemming. Each played a central role in the administration's handling of civil rights issues. One of the most interesting discussions during the panel session involved Maxwell Rabb's review of the desegration efforts of the Eisenhower Administration. Maxwell Rabb describes the climate in 1953 when the "separate but equal" facilities rule was the law of the land as a result of a fifty-year-old Supreme Court decision. In 1896 the Supreme Court established in *Plessy v. Ferguson* that separate but equal was an acceptable doctrine. This doctrine allowed a host of public facilities to continue to be segregated, including public schools.

President Eisenhower was strongly opposed to the doctrine of separate by equal, but could not directly go against a Supreme Court decision. Ambassador Rabb chronicles the early efforts by

President Eisenhower to combat segregation in spite of the *Plessy* decision. So effective and thorough were President Eisenhower's efforts to achieve desegregation in federal facilities, which were directly under his jurisdiction, that in the 1956 presidential election, Congressman Adam Clayton Powell, a Democrat from Harlem, openly supported the President. Ambassador Rabb also recounts the complex problems that President Eisenhower faced in desegregating Washington, D.C. and the manner in which the President personally moved to manage the process. When the administration wanted to end segregation in the movie theaters of Washington, D.C., Eisenhower called a meeting of the leaders of the film industry at the White House. He told them that racial separation in the theaters had to be stopped. They agreed with the President and moved to carry out his request. His personal intervention in the theater case resulted in numerous other businesses in Washington, D.C. tearing down racial barriers.

Perhaps one of the greatest legacies in civil rights during the Eisenhower administration are the two civil rights acts passed during the Eisenhower years. The Civil Rights Act of 1957 stands today as one of the most important pieces of civil rights legislation ever enacted. The law protected basic voting rights created the Civil Rights Commission, and elevated the Civil Rights Section in the Justice Department to the Civil Rights Division with a much larger staff. President Eisenhower actively pursued enforcement of the Civil Rights Act by appointing federal judges sympathetic to his civil rights position and by increasing the number of federal marshals to over six hundred for enforcement. The 1960 Civil Rights Act broadened the protection in voting rights begun under the 1957 act.

Another key discussion to emerge from this panel involved President Eisenhower's response to the 1954 Supreme Court decision of *Brown v. Topeka Board of Education*. Through the Brown decision, the Supreme Court effectively overturned the decision in *Plessy v. Furguson* which had allowed segregation. The Supreme Court firmly stated in the *Brown* decision that segregation was unconstitutional. This was the first time in the nation's history that the Supreme Court had unequivocally stated that separate but equal was not acceptable and segregation had to be ended "in a timely manner". Attorney General Brownell forcefully argues during the panel session that President Eisenhower was unjustly characterized after the *Brown* decision as slow to enforce desegregation in the public school system. He notes that the Supreme Court ordered school districts to move with "deliberate speed", but did not give a clear view of how much time should be allowed by the federal government. As a result, President Eisenhower could not use the Justice Department for enforcement. Brownell argues that President Eisenhower pursued every avenue within his power to desegregate the schools, but unless the Supreme Court amended its decision, he could not use the full range of his authority. Attorney General Brownell added that when Governor Orval Faubus of Arkansas sought to ignore the Supreme Court ruling and fight desegregation, President Eisenhower sent in federal troops to ensure that black children were admitted into the previously all-white public school. President Eisenhower moved quickly and decisively to resolve the conflict. As Brownell quotes President Eisenhower about his decision to send in the troops to resolve the issue, "I learned from my military experience that if you have to use force, use overwhelming force so that there will be no casualties." The desegregation of the Little Rock High School was carried out without any loss of life.

This panel session provides numerous insights into the strategies that President Eisenhower employed to counter segregation prior to 1954 when the *Plessy* decision governed, and how he moved swiftly to end segregation as soon as the *Plessy* decision was overturned.

PANEL

Moderator: **Robert Burk,** *Professor of History, Muskingum College*

Panelists:

Arthur Flemming   *Secretary of Health, Education and Welfare, 1958-61*

Herbert Brownell   *Attorney General of the United States, 1953-57*

Maxwell Rabb   *Secretary to the Cabinet of President Eisenhower, 1953-58*

Rocco Siciliano   *Special Assistant to President Eisenhower, 1957-59; Assistant Secretary of Labor, 1953-57; Under Secretary of U.S. Department of Commerce, 1969-71*

Robert Burk: I'd like to begin by posing a general question to each of the panelists as a way of getting started this afternoon. What would each of you say was President Eisenhower's guiding philosophy on Civil Rights, particularly as far as the role of the Federal Government in enforcing civil rights? Maxwell.

Maxwell Rabb: There is no question that President Eisenhower was extremely interested in developing progress in the field of civil rights. His guiding principle in all of this was not to be involved in talk but to have action and to see that something was done. He followed, under all conditions, the Constitution of the United States. He never hesitated to take firm steps, such as was demonstrated at Little Rock by having the military make certain that his requests were carried out.

Robert Burk: General Brownell, you had a lot of experience in terms of dealing with those federal-state issues that had an impact on that question. How would you answer that?

Herbert Brownell: Well, I first learned about Eisenhower's philosophy about civil rights when he asked me to come over to Paris when he was at NATO as he was trying to decide whether or not to run for the presidency. As you know, Republicans and

Democrats were begging him to run for president. This was in the early spring of 1952. I had a day-long conference with him at the NATO headquarters and among other things that came up was the question of civil rights. I told him that he would have to face that in the campaign and I asked him what were his views. He started by telling of his experiences as commander-in-chief of the armed forces against Hitler, at which time he took a leading role in removing discrimination between the black troops and the white troops under his command. He said, to summarize this, "I believe, if I were elected President, the first thing I would do was see to it that discrimination was eliminated in every area under Federal jurisdiction." Of course, that was before *Brown v. Board of Education* was decided. In the areas of strictly Federal jurisdiction, he took immediate action to desegregate the capital, Washington, D.C.; to complete the program of eliminating this discrimination in the armed forces, for example, the naval stations; and to set up the Government Contracts Committee, which provided that in every government contract, there should be a clause prohibiting discrimination on the basis of race or color. That was his overriding philosophy. We'll later get to what happened after the Supreme Court acted in *Brown v. the Board of Education.*

Robert Burk: Secretary Flemming, you had a chance to witness President Eisenhower's wrestling of the civil rights question, particularly in the latter stages of his administration when you were Secretary of Health, Education and Welfare. What was your impression of the President's overall views on civil rights.

Arthur Flemming: Well, I also had the opportunity of watching him wrestle these issues right from the beginning of his first term. As General Brownell and Max Rabb know, I was in the Cabinet then as Director of the Office of Defense Mobilization. I remember very distinctly a Cabinet discussion relative to how we, as an Executive Branch, should respond to *Brown v. Board of Education,* and what we should submit to the Congress in the way of proposed legislation. I'd sum it up this way. As I recall, right at the beginning of his administration, he sent a note to then-Director of the Budget, Joe Dodge, in which he said he wanted his administration to be characterized as an administration that would move forward in connection with programs dealing with the welfare of people. He stressed that he didn't expect any giant leaps forward, but he wanted a consistent forward movement. As I watched him deal with issues in the field of civil rights, I felt that was his approach to civil rights. He wanted to see the nation move forward, and he created the kind of climate that was a challenge to those of us who were a part of his administration to help him achieve that kind of an objective.

Robert Burk: Mr. Siciliano, you have another unique perspective, really a dual perspective, on this because, for a time in this administration, you served under Cabinet officer, James Mitchell, who was, I know, very concerned and dedicated to civil rights. Then you moved over to the White House where the staff was very much involved in civil rights issues. How would you view Eisenhower on civil rights?

Rocco Siciliano: I can't add too much to what has already been said, but I'd like to talk about his own fundamental sense of decency. I think that we should all remember that decency is really what governs anyone in any position of prominence or power; and he certainly held both those positions. At the same time, we have to remember that in 1953, when he took office, there was total segregation in the United States. It's very hard, except for those of us who are senior citizens today, to remember what the climate was like in 1953. The climate at that time said that the so called "separate but equal" facilities was the law. It was a law that was then almost 85 years in passing. It was a Supreme Court law in a sense. He had to combat what he thought was the "then" law with what he felt was right, and that was what he attempted to tackle over the next eight years.

Robert Burk: All of you, I think, have mentioned at one point or another about how initially he was very much interested in fulfilling the desegregation in the Armed Forces, and in moving on desegregation in the District of Columbia. Why were those areas the immediate focus? Would you talk a little bit about the problems even where you did have a clearer federal jurisdiction.

Maxwell Rabb: The first civil rights problem in the Eisenhower Administration was the Thompson Restaurant case and it was General Brownell, as Attorney General, who successfully resolved this discrimination matter in the court room. It immediately paved the way in the District of Columbia to end the practice of segregation in the restaurants there.

Shortly thereafter, the desegregation issue came to a head with Congressman Adam Clayton Powell's vigorous criticism of President Eisenhower for failing to move expeditiously to eliminate discrimination in the Veterans' hospitals, at the Naval bases, and in the Defense establishment. The President, at that point, assigned me to take over the area of civil rights in the White House in addition to my other official duties there. So effective and thorough were Dwight D. Eisenhower's efforts in these matters and several other aspects of the fight to achieve desegregation that in the 1956 presidential election, Congressman Powell, a Democrat from Harlem, openly supported Eisenhower.

In early 1953, the President gave me the assignment of directing the project of completely eliminating segregation in Washington D.C. He told me, "I do not want to follow the approach of my recent predecessors who concentrated on achieving favorable publicity by resorting to talk. I want results. They annually urged legislation to outlaw the poll-tax or anti-lynching or F.E.P.C. reform, knowing full well that the result would be harsh words and a venting of anger with no progress at the end. There would be a 30 or a 60 or a 90 day filibuster in Congress with nothing accomplished at the end. We cannot afford that; we must move ahead. And let us do it quietly and effectively so that there will be a record of accomplishment."

This was the formula that was followed and it was an approach that brought about significant achievements in civil rights. For example, desegregation in the Nation's capital was completely realized by an intense and concentrated campaign. It involved 52 separate areas of life and government in the District of Columbia to accomplish the effort. In 1954, Ralph Bunche visited with President Eisenhower at the White House. He made the statement that, when President Truman was there he had offered Bunche the position of Assistant Secretary of State. He declined saying that he could not have his family live in a segregated Washington. He went on to state, "Today, if that post were offered to me and the situation was right otherwise, I would certainly accept it because you, President Eisenhower, have completely desegregated the city of Washington."

Robert Burk: Ambassador Rabb mentioned the Thompson case.

Herbert Brownell: Well, it's hard to recall now and hard to explain to a student of the present day that, when Eisenhower walked into Washington as President, a black citizen could not get a meal at a Washington, D.C. restaurant. He couldn't go to the theater; he couldn't go to any of the public swimming pools. Washington, D.C. was a southern town, governed really by a committee of the Congress made up mostly of southern Senators and Congressmen. This was before Home Rule for the District of Columbia. That was the situation that faced Eisenhower when he was inaugurated President.

One of his first appointees was Sam Spencer as the Commissioner of the District of Columbia. He told him that, since the District was under federal jurisdiction, he didn't require any legislation from Congress, and didn't have to undergo a filibuster, he wanted to completely desegregate the Nation's capital. There was, in fact, a law on the books that had been passed shortly after the Civil War, which abolished segregation in Washington, D.C., but they had never enforced it. He asked the commissioners of the District about it and they said, "Well, that's a lost statute. Nothing's been done under that for eighty-five years, so we just forgot about it." Then the President asked me about the matter and what my opinion was as to whether or not that municipal statute was still in force. I advised him that it was. He said, "You take charge of the case." There was a case pending in court to test this out. So, he superseded the corporation counsel of the District of Columbia, asked us to take charge of that case, and the court upheld our view that it was a valid statute. Then he called in all the leading citizens of the Washington, D.C. community and told them that he wanted hotels to be desegregated, the restaurants to be desegregated, the swimming pools, the theaters, everything. And they responded. During the first year of his administration, with citizen cooperation, he completely desegregated Washington, D.C.

Maxwell Rabb: I agree that President Eisenhower personally participated often and directly to achieve an end to discrimination. I recall when we had to end segregation in the theaters of the District of Columbia, he did not hesitate to call together at the White House the famed leaders of the film industry to help him: Louis B. Meyer, Spyros Skouras, Adolph Zukor, and Barney Balaban among others. He told them that racial separation in the movie houses had to be stopped and they enthusiastically moved into action and carried out the President's request.

Arthur Flemming: I might just add, I moved to Washington right out of college in 1927. I got there ahead of my three colleagues here, but what General Brownell has described is completely accurate. I can assure you it was a very, very discouraging city to live in, and it was very exciting to be a part of an administration where the President would actually exercise the authority that he had in the way in which he exercised it.

Robert Burk: Talking about the Thompson case reminds me that one of the cases that was part of the Brown package involved a District of Columbia school desegregation case, so let me move into the subject of the Brown decision. What do you think was the President's view on the constitutionality of segregated schools at the time? Did you feel, General Brownell, that you were getting the kind of support you wanted from the President in preparing the briefs for the Supreme Court?

Herbert Brownell: Well, the Brown case had been argued in the Supreme Court before Eisenhower had been inaugurated as President, but instead of deciding the case, the court announced that it was scheduling it for re-argument in the following year. The Attorney General was invited to write a brief on the subject of the constitutionality of segregation in the schools and to prepare and argue the case. So, obviously before they acted, the Court wanted to know public sentiment throughout the community and the nation. They also wanted to hear the views of the Eisenhower Administration. I went to Eisenhower and said, "They have asked me to appear in the case. What's your thought on it?" He said, "Under the separation of powers, this is a job for the Supreme Court. We're not a party in the case. This is a case between the school children and their parents and the local boards of education." The federal government was not a party to the *Brown v. the Board of Education* case. I said, "The Court has asked us to appear and I think it would be very bad for relations between the Executive Branch and the Court if we didn't respond affirmatively and appear in the case." He accepted that recommendation and we agreed to accept the Court's invitation. Then the question came up as to what would be our response. And on that, Eisenhower said, "Let the Court decide it." I said, "We are now before the Court and they will ask us the questions: Is segregation in the schools constitutional? Shall we overturn the *Plessy v. Ferguson* ruling which is the old case which allowed segregation in the schools and had been the law of the land, under the Supreme Court, ever since the 1880's?" Several generations of people have been brought up under the ruling that the *Plessy v. Ferguson* case allowed segregation in the schools. He said, "So you have to answer the question?" And I said, "Yes." "Well," he said, "what is your opinion on constitutionality in the schools?" I said, "Well, my professional opinion is that it is unconstitutional to continue segregation in the schools." He said, and this was so typical of the delegation of authority that he gave to his Cabinet members and to his assistants, "That is your professional opinion? Then, if the Court asks you the question, you tell them what your opinion is;" and that was the decision that he made at that time. We went before the Court and when the question was asked from the bench, we stated our professional opinion that segregation was unconstitutional.

Arthur Flemming: I would like to say that the conversation you have just narrated is one of the most important conversations that has taken place in the history of the Civil Rights movement. I'm going to jump ahead a little bit on your chronology here. Later on, we'll talk about the Civil Rights Act of 1957, and the fact that it created a Commission on Civil Rights, a Commission which I had the privilege of chairing for eight years.

Robert Burk: Yes, with great distinction.

Arthur Flemming: Now, after those eight years as Chair of the U. S. Commission on Civil Rights, I have a far deeper appreciation of the significance of that conversation than I would have had without having that experience. We owe you and President Eisenhower a great debt because of the way that conversation turned out.

Robert Burk: How much of that was actually discussed at the Cabinet level or was this more or less a decision that you and the President talked about, General? I'm just wondering to what extent the Cabinet as a whole was giving input as to what extent this should be an administration position and to what extent you may have felt pros and cons from different voices in the administration?

Herbert Brownell: That decision was never brought before the Cabinet.

Robert Burk: Some have suggested, so I'm going to play devil's advocate here and throw this out for all of you...

Arthur Flemming: So, you say the proposed Civil Rights Act of 1957 didn't come before the Cabinet?

Herbert Brownell: Yes.

Robert Burk: Let me play devil's advocate and throw out something for all of you to respond to. Once the Brown decision came out and President Eisenhower said, "This is the law of the land, it must and shall be enforced," there was criticism in some quarters. They would have preferred a more positive endorsement of the principles in Brown and the President perhaps should have used his office as a "bully pulpit" somewhat more than he did. Does anyone want to take on that one?

Rocco Siciliano: That's a tough one because this is a question of moral leadership and that's really what is behind that question. There were certainly those in the black community who felt that the President should speak out quickly and easily in favor, from the moral point of view, of desegregation; not just in the schools, although this was the first issue of 1957. The Civil Rights Commission then was created basically for school desegregation, not for other forms of desegregation which followed later and were actually put into law in 1964, when Mr. Johnson was President. The President, himself, in my judgment, could only go so far. He supported the decision of the Supreme Court in a personal way, but he did not really reveal any support until he wrote his memoirs after he left office. Now that can create, particularly in the minds of the civil rights activists, a great irritation with them because they felt that he should use this "bully pulpit" thing. But his attitude was, and it was a pragmatic attitude, that he was enveloped by a history of his own. After all, he had been a military man, he saw the intense bubbling and dissention that was going on in the United States, and he knew very well that this could lead to a kind of insurrection, if you want to call it that. It's a very strong word. He felt very clear in his own mind that he was not going to be using the presidency as a pulpit, and you have to live with that. You can agree with it or you can disagree with it, but that was his position.

Herbert Brownell: Well, I can add to that. I think he, as Ambassador Rabb said in the very beginning, was a man of action rather than words. So when the second Brown decision came down, the first thing that he did was to order the desegregation of the schools in the District of Columbia. That was under the federal government's jurisdiction; and the year after the Brown decision came down, the public schools in the District of Columbia complied in every way with the Brown decision and were completely desegregated.

Robert Burk: That wasn't an easy call either, was it? Washington was such a southern city in many respects.

Rocco Siciliano: It really was. Washington *was* a southern city. I didn't go there in 1927 when Arthur did, but I went to law school there after World War II. It was a shock for somebody from Utah to come and see people standing in a Woolworth's waiting to get in, trying to get food. They were all blacks, and all the seats on the left hand side were empty. I didn't realize what this was all about. That was outlawed very quickly once he took office. I don't think we should throw rocks although it's easy to do so from a historian's point of view. I've seen some of the current histories, I couldn't name names, which simply take him to task for not using his presidency as a pulpit. By not understanding what the mood and the temperament of the country was at the time, it's easy now, with hindsight, to take him to task for this, as several very good books on the subject do nevertheless.

Maxwell Rabb: I think Rocco Siciliano has said it very well. I must draw attention to the fact that President Eisenhower believed in getting something done, not in words. This entire question, I think, could be summed up in what took place at Little Rock. He moved quickly and he moved in a very firm way. He was criticized for that, but let me tell you, in the long run, what counts is not just phrases piled on phrases but on action piled on action. He did what the law and his duty told him was correct. History has given him a verdict of approval.

Rocco Siciliano: May I read his own words?

Maxwell Rabb: Certainly, Rocco.

Rocco Siciliano: I think his own words help here with respect to the moral leadership question. This was in 1959 and I think it says best what he himself thinks because this is what he wrote: "If it's going to be true to its own founding documents, the United States government does have the job of working toward the time when there is no discrimination made on such inconsequential reasons as race, color or religion." And then he added this, "Law is not going to do it. We have never stopped sin by passing laws. And in the same way, we are not going to take a great moral idea and achieve it merely by law." Now, you may not agree with all of this, but this was his point of view. Education, in his mind, was the answer to changing the hearts of the people.

Arthur Flemming: I have often asked this same question, and I feel that normally his response was that he felt as President of the United States, when it came to Supreme Court decisions, it was his job to enforce them. He also felt that if he got into the business of evaluating Supreme Court decisions, either pro or con, it would interfere with his ability to implement those decisions in an effective way. *(Turning to Gen. Brownell)* Now, I'm sure he talked with you about that a good many times. That was at the heart, wasn't it, of a position he took relative to...

Herbert Brownell: That's correct. One intervening fact that most historians so far have overlooked, is that there were two Brown cases, Brown One and Brown Two. The second Brown case told how it should be enforced. When we filed the brief with the Justice Department, we advocated that it should be left to the local courts to consider plans for desegregation that would vary in different parts of the country, depending on the local facts. We said every plan must be filed within ninety days, so that there could be prompt enforcement machinery from the Department of Justice to move into action and enforce *Brown v. the Board of Education.* The Supreme Court rejected that approach. Instead of saying that the plan should be filed right away (we thought it should), they said we should move with all deliberate speed. That was the famous decision of the Court. Now in the south, where they opposed that decision, they took that as meaning "whenever you get around to it." They were going to be a lot more deliberate than anybody else. That posed a terrible enforcement problem for Ike and for his administration because there was no statute that gave the Department of Justice the authority to move in and desegregate the schools. It had to be done pursuant to an order of the local district courts; and that might be "manana," or it might be five years from now. Eisenhower always resented people who said, "Why don't you get out there and enforce *Brown v. Board of Education* when the Court itself had laid down the law that it was to let the courts move with all deliberate speed here." That's when he first expressed the view, as it has already been stated here, that it wasn't enough to have a Supreme Court decision. It wasn't enough to have a statute, although there were no statutes, but it was a combination of law enforcement and public education. He's the one who predicted the situation that we have today, thirty years later; and it has taken at least a generation, and maybe more, before we eliminate discrimination from society. I think that he always felt that the criticism that you have described here was unfair when you look at how his hands were tied by the Court itself as to immediate enforcement of the case.

Robert Burk: I suppose we ought to mention at this point that one key aspect, which leads up to the *Brown* decision anyway, is the appointment of Justice Warren. Imagine how different things would have been without Justice Warren on the bench.

Arthur Flemming: I'd like to follow up on that particular comment because you've put your finger on a very important contribution that he made. I was interested that all three of my colleagues have drawn this distinction between some words or thoughts that President Eisenhower might have used at a particular time, and his actions. Of course, when I became Secretary of Health, Education and Welfare, I got into some interesting dialogues with him on the role of the federal government in the field of education. He was rather reluctant to move as far as some of us thought we should move in that particular area, but he would always listen. That's where we had some very interesting discussions in the Cabinet, and from time to time he would give us a green light to move in those particular areas. Then he'd make some comments that were not necessarily the most supportive comments for that particular proposal. He'd revert to some of his philosophy as far as the role of the federal government in the field of education was concerned, but he had given us a green light for action. He wouldn't pull back on that at all. We had the opportunity of going up and trying to persuade Congress that the time had come for action.

Robert Burk: How much of that do you think is unconscious? How much of it is conscious—this tendency to go back? I have sometimes wondered when I've looked at the Civil Rights legislation that was presented in 1956. It's as if, in some ways, the President is giving you the go-ahead but he's preserving flexibility for himself to back up a little bit if need be. Is that fair?

Rocco Siciliano: Well, let me talk about the local law... comments from Maxwell Rabb...go ahead.

Maxwell Rabb: The one thing that's bothered me about this entire discussion is that we have largely concentrated on the *Brown* decision so that it has obscured Eisenhower's many considerable contributions to the cause of civil rights. The *Brown* decision was important but it must distant and diminish the many anti-discrimination achievements he brought about during his two terms as President. There was one civil rights accomplishment after another. I have no hesitancy in saying that his record in this respect was as good, if not better, than that of any other American President in modern times. Please remember, he did all this in a period in which civil rights advocacy had not reached its highest point of intensity and activism.

We must put into proper perspective the great strides that were quietly and effectively made during Eisenhower's Administration. We have mentioned the desegregation of the Nation's capital. There were two vital Commissions, the Committee on Contract Compliance and the Committee on Employment, that were given for the first time Presidential level with the Vice President as Chairman and the Secretary of Labor as the Vice Chairman. The naval bases were desegregated, the schools on the military bases were ordered to end discrimination, as were 48 veterans' hospitals. The first civil rights legislation since the Civil War was passed and Little Rock was a landmark for future generations. Yes, it was a good record indeed.

Rocco Siciliano: What I wanted to do was to remind people that with the 1957 act, which was the first of the civil rights pieces that passed, there wasn't unanimity in the civil rights community. Jackie Robinson, a very famous black baseball player, as most of you in our age group will remember and Philip Randolph, who was the acknowledged black leader, at least at that time, the "Old Lion" as he was called, both recommended to the President that he veto that piece of legislation because they thought it did not go far enough. On the other hand, the Reverend Martin Luther King recommended that he sign it. The black community was divided, so the unanimity that we talk about was not there. There was such total diversity in the civil rights community. They were not always just black, by the way. We think that when the President got this on his desk *bang*—he went ahead and signed it. This is not the case. He was urged strongly by some to veto it.

Arthur Flemming: *To Robert Burk.* You made mention to Chief Justice Warren. I'd like to make one point that I've made many, many times out of your presence and I'd like to make it in your presence. I feel that possibly the outstanding and most lasting contribution that the Eisenhower administration made to the civil rights movement was its strict adherence to high standards in appointments to the Federal Judiciary. Some of you may have had the opportunity of reading a book entitled *Unlikely Heroes* by Jack Bass, in which he describes the dramatic story of a southern judge of the Fifth Circuit who translated the Supreme Court's *Brown* Decision into a revolution for equality. But if you read that book, you'll find ten to fifteen references in the book to Herbert Brownell and the role that he played in finding some of these judges and persuading the President of the United States to appoint them. As you read that book, you can gather right away that it was a team operation. The President obviously relied very heavily on the Attorney General's judgment but he wanted to meet with all of them, he wanted to talk with all of them. He apparently had certain questions that he addressed to all of them, but as a result of the leadership that we received from Herbert Brownell during that

period of time, we not only have the appointment of Earl Warren, and a gentleman whose retirement we have noted with
great regret recently, Justice Brennan, but many U.S. district
judges who later became circuit judges. I can assure you that
one could not serve, as I did, under the Civil Rights Commission, and read opinion after opinion of these people without
knowing that they were the people who *really* put the civil
rights movement in this country on a solid foundation. I'm sad
to say that there hasn't been that same strict adherence to high
standards in recent years and we may have some difficulties
ahead as a result of that. But I feel that that's a tremendous contribution that President Eisenhower, with the help of Herbert
Brownell, made to the civil rights movement.

Rocco Siciliano: You're so right. I don't think that Herbert Brownell's role has really been properly appreciated. I said
this in June in Abilene, Kansas, and I'm happy to piggyback on
Arthur Flemming's statements.

Robert Burk: You had to take a good deal of heat, I would
imagine, on some of those appointments given Senatorial
courtesy. I guess we would be remiss if we didn't address Little
Rock, albeit briefly under the time constraints.

The President's great desire was to avoid the use of coer-
cive federal force against southern authority, and yet he found
he had to do it at Little Rock. That had to have been an incre-
dibly difficult time, politically and personally, for the President
and for those of you there at the time.

Herbert Brownell: It was very difficult for President
Eisenhower. After the second *Brown* decision, there were 103
members of Congress who signed what they called the "southern manifesto" which said they would use all means within
their power to see to it that *Brown v. Board of Education* was
never enforced. They followed that up with the formation
throughout the south of what they called White Citizens Councils who were dedicated to seeing to it that segregation continued in the schools. It all came to a focus at Little Rock and
here was another illustration of the point that we've been making here—Eisenhower, when necessary to act, acted. When
somebody asked him at a press conference if he was going to
send in the troops, he said, "Why, I wouldn't think of it. I can't

imagine any circumstances under which I would use federal troops to enforce *Brown v. Board of Education;*" but, he never envisioned the fact that the governor of a sovereign state, i.e. Governor Orval Faubus of Arkansas, although he had taken an oath of office to support the Constitution, would defy it, which he did. Faubus called out the Arkansas National Guard which was, of course, under his control as governor, ringed it around the high school at Little Rock, and, by force, prevented the black children from entering the school.

Robert Burk: Did President Eisenhower believe that he had gotten a firm enough pledge from Governor Faubus at Newport? Did he feel Faubus really had gone back on his assurances?

Herbert Brownell: Well, I can testify to a certain extent on that. I didn't think it would work for President Eisenhower to meet with Faubus, because I had dealt with Faubus for several months; but he decided he'd make one last effort to settle this constitutional crisis peaceably. He met with Faubus up in Rhode Island at Newport and they went into a huddle, just the two of them, without anyone to take notes or observe. When they came out and, in my presence, the President said, "Well, Governor Faubus and I have agreed that the black children can enter the high school," I was really astounded but very happy at the outcome. But Faubus went back to Arkansas and consulted with his political managers. He was running for re-election that year for governor, and they told him that if he allowed the black children into the high school, he could not be re-elected. So, he changed his mind and kept the troops, the National Guard of Arkansas, around the high school. Well, when President Eisenhower found out about it, he exhibited one of his strong, famous fits of anger and he called me from Washington and said, "Well, you were right, he's double-crossed me and I'm going to see to it that integration is enforced there. I'm coming to Washington and I'll make a speech to the Nation"—which he did. The first thing that Faubus or anybody else knew, the 101st Airborne Division, with bayonets over their shoulders, were walking up the main street of Little Rock. As you know, they stayed there that whole school year and saw to it that the black children were allowed to enter and stay there and attend classes for the rest of that year.

Now, thirty years later at Abilene, just this summer, Faubus and I and four of the black children were on the same platform talking about Little Rock. Faubus spoke first and they said, well, what do you think? And he said, "If I had to do it all over again, I'd do the same thing." The black children then testified as to what they were up against in those days after they were allowed to go to school—all the harassment, the insults and whatnot that they had to face. It brought back to my mind how magnificently the black children acted in the face of those obstacles. I also recalled that after Eisenhower said, "I'll have to send in the troops," he told me, "I learned from my military experience that if you have to use force, use overwhelming force so that there will be no casualties." So, the desegregation of the Little Rock High School was carried out without any loss of life.

Rocco Siciliano: What we've also forgotten, just to show how unrepentant Governor Faubus was, is that federal troops were kept in Central High School through the end of that school year. The following September of 1958, the Governor closed the high school entirely so that he not only punished the nine black students, but he punished all the other hundreds of kids who were white, who were also going to that school. He closed the school, and it stayed closed for another year until it was then re-opened on an integrated basis. I think so often people forget that little postscript. That's just how he felt, as we heard [from General Brownell], and I was also in Abilene when the statement was made in June—he hasn't changed his mind.

Arthur Flemming: I'll also testify as to what that did to set a climate as far as the Eisenhower Administration was concerned. In 1957, I was not in office but I came back in 1958, as Secretary of Health, Education and Welfare. I had a press conference every other Monday morning. Soon after I came back, in Prince William County in Northern Virginia, they decided to close all of their public schools and provide vouchers and funds for the parents so that they could put their children into segregated schools. Arkansas put into effect a somewhat similar program; but this one was focused on Virginia. I got a question as to what I thought about it and, more specifically, whether or not we were going to let any federal money go into those segregated schools. Well, I didn't have any difficulty in expressing my views as to the policy of what impact that was going to have on the lives of minority children, but I also didn't have any hesitancy in saying, "No, there will be no federal money going in there." Now I didn't check with anybody before I said that, I didn't call your successor, Bill Rogers, I didn't call the White House or anything of the kind. I knew I was working for an administration that wouldn't tolerate this, so I had no hesitancy in making that statement kind of "off the cuff."

Robert Burk: I, obviously, wish we had a lot more time and I suspect the audience does too because this has been fascinating.

Kenneth Holland: I'm Kenneth Holland from the University of Vermont, and I just wanted to ask your views of the apocryphal quotation that's often attributed to President Eisenhower when he was asked at the end of the second term, "Mr. President, did you make any mistakes while you were President?" Supposedly he said, "Yes, two, and they're both sitting on the Supreme Court."

Robert Burk: The question was what the response of the panelists is regarding the statement attributed to President Eisenhower at the end of his presidency that he had made two mistakes and both of them were on the Supreme Court.

Herbert Brownell: Well, I think it is apocryphal. I researched it in some depth, and the first time it was printed in a book, I asked the author where he got the story. He said, "I read it in the newspaper." Recently there was a young lady researcher in New Jersey, I'm sorry to say I don't even know her name, who tried to research it because Justice Brennan had just retired from the Supreme Court. They transferred this story then instead of saying that "Earl Warren was the worst appointment I ever made." They then attributed to Eisenhower "Bill Brennan was the worst appointment that I ever made." Well, we had it both ways; but she checked up and she found out that this was an old joke that public officials, including Presidents, always used. Some disgruntled person would come to the President and say, "Why did you ever appoint that fellow?" The President would always say, "That's the worst mistake I ever made." Of course, he was trying to be friendly. I don't think that

Eisenhower ever said it. He certainly didn't ever say it publicly, it's against all of his nature to do that. Earl Warren and Bill Brennan in their time denied that they ever heard the story, so I think the questioner here is right. It's an apocryphal story that's lots of fun to tell but didn't happen.

Robert Shogan: My name is Robert Shogan and I'm a reporter for the *Los Angeles Times,* Washington Bureau. My question is also for General Brownell. Reference was made to Eisenhower's statement at the press conference that he couldn't conceive sending troops in to enforce school desegregation. In your opinion, General, from the conversations you had with Faubus and from your overall efforts in the area, were Faubus and other southern politicians mindful of that statement? Did that influence their actions? Did that influence their conduct? Did that make them think that Ike would be reluctant to enforce the court order?

Robert Burk: The question was, given President Eisenhower's statement which I believe came two months before Little Rock, that he couldn't imagine any set of circumstances that would cause him to use federal troops to enforce a court order; did that give encouragement to southern politicians such as Governor Faubus to obstruct because they didn't think that the federal government would respond? What are your feelings on that?

Herbert Brownell: Well, of course, I couldn't answer for Governor Faubus. He and I were never too close. But you have to remember the setting in which the statement was made. The Civil Rights Act of 1957 was under hearings before Congress at that time and the southern Senators were saying every day, every hour on the hour, that the Civil Rights Act of 1957 was just a scheme by which Eisenhower expected to enforce *Brown v. Board of Education* by sending troops into the south. The southern Senators felt the administration would have another reconstruction era, another force—"Carpetbaggers"—in the south. They were going to supersede the governors and the school boards and occupy the south with federal troops. So Eisenhower said, and he meant it, that he couldn't conceive of any circumstances under which he would use federal troops to enforce the Brown decision; but he never envisioned that a governor of a sovereign state would defy the Constitution. When he was faced with actuality and there was, in effect, rebellion against the *Brown* decision in interpreting the Constitution, he didn't hesitate to do his duty under the Constitution and enforce the law.

George Wills: I worked with Milton Eisenhower for a number of years at Johns Hopkins University and would like to add a footnote to this subject. Martin Luther King spoke at Johns Hopkins in about 1967, at the time of great fervor in the civil rights movement. At that time, President Eisenhower was in the hospital and Dr. King sought out Milt Eisenhower after the speech. I still remember the speech in a very crowded auditorium at Hopkins; the kids were just hanging "off the rafters." It was a very powerful speech. He [King] sought Dr. Eisenhower out and we got the two of them together in the back of the auditorium. He said, "I just want you to give my special regards to your brother. He really got it all started, and he and Attorney General Brownell made so much happen that has given us the momentum." I think this panel today supplements that, because it was a remarkable exchange between those two men at a point when the perspective was there; and this panel was very reinforcing in that connection. King put it right on the line with Milton when he made that comment, which was a very special thing to hear in light of all the challenges that were facing him at that time concerning the civil rights issue.

Rocco Siciliano: I would like to comment on that. I'm very happy to hear that, because I'm asked the question having to do with the one and only meeting President Eisenhower had with the black leader, which I was, frankly, somewhat responsible for—at least in talking with Martin Luther King and setting it up along with the first black professional person in the White House, Fred Morrow. I'm sorry he's not here today, he's in the hospital. Fred should be here because he deserves so much credit. In any case, we had that meeting on June 23, 1958. It was the first meeting that black leaders had ever had of this kind, certainly with President Eisenhower. It was a rare occurence, but it was also, in a sense, a summit meeting. It was that meeting, more than any one thing in my judgment, which established Martin Luther King as a truly national leader. He was well-known, he was very effective and he had a White House podium in 1958. He met with the President along with A. Philip Randolph, Lester Granger and Roy Wilkins, and instead of meeting for thirty minutes, they met for fifty minutes. It was without doubt a very eventful occurrence for them as black leaders.

George Wills: He spoke with great emotion when he spoke to Milton Eisenhower about that. I can still see him grabbing both of his arms and he said, "Tell your brother I said hello. He and Attorney General Brownell got it all started." There was a real sense of reality there.

Jim Riddlesperger: Hi, I'm Jim Riddlesperger of Texas Christian University. I have a question which I think may be for General Brownell, but maybe the rest of you would know the answer.

The 1957 Civil Rights Act, which I really wish we could have talked a little bit more about today, is something that's very interesting. Not only was it an opportunity for President Eisenhower to make, with your help, a fairly strong statement about four provisions that he thought would be important to have civil rights; it was also a terrific legislative struggle. It was a legislative struggle because it was led in part by Lyndon Johnson. What I want to know is what was Eisenhower's true feeling about Johnson's role in this; and particularly, what was his feeling about the trade-off of Section Three of that Bill or the jury trial amendment that was added?

Robert Burk: The question has to do with the relationship between President Eisenhower and Senate Majority Leader Johnson, particularly with regard to the 1957 Civil Rights legislation. What was the President's attitude toward Johnson's role in that legislation, both in terms of its effect on Part III of the Bill and then the jury trial amendment that was attached?

Herbert Brownell: This is an important part of the civil rights story of the Eisenhower Administration. It illustrates the fact that President Eisenhower delegated great authority to his Cabinet officers and to his assistants, and he expected them to come up with solutions to problems in their areas. And so, the chief problem that we had in the Justice Department was that there was no real enforcement statute for civil rights on the books. We developed the four-part bill which established the Civil Rights Commission, raised the Civil Rights Section in the Department of Justice to a full division with appropriation, established federal machinery to enforce voting rights for black citizens, and provided that the Attorney General had the authority to enforce any civil right that the Supreme Court declared to be one of the civil rights enforceable under the Constitution. We went to the Congress with that bill, that four-point bill, and in the 1956 re-election campaign President Eisenhower endorsed the bill. We tried to get it through the Congress. It passed the House and then went to the Senate. Of course, civil rights bills ever since the Civil War had been buried in the Senate by filibuster in the Judiciary Committee. The Chairman was James Eastland of Mississippi, a great civil rights advocate, as I remember! *(This remark was accompanied by laughter, giving the impression of sarcasm.)* When the bill was passed by the House, we arranged to have it taken by courier to the desk of Vice President Nixon, who was presiding over the Senate. By arrangement between him and Republican Senate Leader William Knowland of California, Nixon announced that, instead of referring the bill to the graveyard Judiciary Committee, he would refer it directly to the floor of the Senate. And that's the way the Civil Rights Act of 1957 came to be voted upon.

Well, when the bill was debated on the floor of the Senate, they denounced Nixon, they denounced me, they denounced everybody for violating the Senate rule and bringing it up for floor debate without going through a committee. Lyndon Johnson went to the President and said, "I have enough votes that, if you leave Point III in the bill, the one giving power to the Attorney General to generally enforce civil rights, the bill will be killed." Eisenhower knew, of course, that he [Johnson] had the majority of votes in the Senate, and he agreed to drop Section III of the Bill. As he explained in later years, the reason he did that was because it was the only way he could salvage the remainder of the bill. The important parts to be salvaged were (1) voting rights for black citizens to be enforced in the Federal courts, (2) establishment of the Civil Rights Commission, (3) establishment of a Civil Rights Division in the Department of Justice. Under the circumstances, it was the only thing that he could do. Stripped of this one section, the Bill passed. Johnson had tried to emasculate the bill by adding to it the so-called jury trial amendment. He had tried to trade off votes against our bill in exchange for our votes to build a power dam in the northwest. In this way, he hoped he could get some votes from the Senators representing the northwestern states. After all that obstruction and stripping Section III from the Bill, he announced that, despite a hard fight on his part, he had passed the first civil rights bill since the Civil War.

CHAPTER FOUR

Domestic Policy and the Eisenhower Legacy

In order to examine the Eisenhower legacy in domestic policy, the Eisenhower Symposium brought together not only key members of the Eisenhower administration but key members of later administrations. Each of the participants provided an insider's view of how the Eisenhower domestic policy agenda was shaped, and how later administrations reshaped or maintained those policies. One of the major changes made by the Eisenhower administration in domestic policy was the manner in which policy itself was developed. President Eisenhower institutionalized a policy making process which fostered internal debate between those staff people who supported a policy and those who opposed it. It was a tough, rigorous, candid debate in which the President took part. He was aware of the different positions, the pros and cons of each issue, and made his decision with this information in hand.

Later Presidents pursued this same staff system. As James Cannon, President Ford's domestic policy advisor, notes on the panel, President Ford used the Eisenhower system of rigorous internal debate. Mr. Cannon notes, however, that President Kennedy did not use the system at the beginning of his administration thus providing one explanation for the Bay of Pigs fiasco. Following the Bay of Pigs, President Kennedy quickly changed his policy-making system to be more in line with that used by President Eisenhower.

Robert C. Wood, Secretary of Housing and Urban Development under President Johnson, points out in his discussion that President Eisenhower provided the structure to "do" domestic policy. Eisenhower enhanced the capacity of the executive office and restored the Council of Economic Advisors to a position of stature. President Eisenhower created a staff system within the White House to pursue domestic policy in a manner no other President had allowed.

Among the numerous domestic policies pursued during the Eisenhower Administration, the creation of the interstate highway system stands out as one of the most distinguished. That system moved goods across its 41,000 mile system and tied the country together as a national network. Dr. Wood argues during the panel discussion that this national transportation system reduced the nation's overall costs and was a major contributor to economic progress during the 1950's.

Another landmark piece of domestic legislation during the Eisenhower administration was the National Defense Education Act. This was the first legislation in over one hundred and fifty years of federal funding for education in which the federal government had provided funds for post secondary education. President Eisenhower aggressively pursued the passage and funding of that bill. Eisenhower was committed to improving the nation's educational level, particularly in mathematics and the sciences, and to make the nation's science internationally competitive.

Major policy initiatives in anti-trust legislation, agricultural subsidies, civil rights, labor relations, health care, and education were among the many accomplishments of the Eisenhower Administration. However, as noted earlier, the staff system set in place by President Eisenhower encouraged new ideas and fostered their development through an organized policy formation process. President Eisenhower referred to this staff system as one whose "purpose is to simplify, clarify, expedite, and coordinate; it is a bulwark against chaos, confusion, delay and failure."

PANEL

Moderator: David Kozak, *Gannon University*

Panelists:

Arthur Flemming   *Secretary of Health, Education and Welfare, 1958-61*

Robert C. Wood   *Secretary of Housing and Urban Development, 1968-69*

James Cannon   *Assistant to the President for Domestic Affairs, 1974-76*

Ralph Bledsoe   *Executive Secretary, Domestic Policy Council, 1985-88*

Herbert Brownell   *Attorney General of the United States, 1953-57*

Rocco Siciliano   *Special Assistant to President Eisenhower, 1957-59; Assistant Secretary of Labor, 1953-57; Under Secretary of U.S. Department of Commerce, 1969-71*

David Kozak: Ladies and gentlemen, it really is my honor to preside over this very distinguished panel this morning which will explore a very important topic. The topic, of course, is the Eisenhower administration and its domestic policy legacy. Too frequently, in the quick histories and studies of the Eisenhower Presidency, we're apt to stress international and national security, the achievements and accomplishments and the legacies in the foreign policy realm; for it was the time of the Cold War and a time of great challenge and significant action with monumental decisions that, in many ways, shaped the world for years to come. The same can also be said of domestic policy and economic policy. Although today, we now all agree that they really aren't separate realms; these issues are intertwined; that most of the major issues of the day are best described as "intermestic." Perhaps this was a time when we could compartmentalize, at least analytically, a bit more comfortably than we can now.

But, to be sure, on the domestic front and in the domestic realm, there is a legacy. There were important decisions, there were important actions. If for no other reason, the Eisenhower Presidency marks a time when the modern presidency had to confront the achievement, the accumulation, the construction of a huge social service bureaucracy; of a growing government with enhanced regulatory power that was the result of America's involvement in World War II, efforts to combat and counteract the Great Depression, and with new governmental action added to it by the Fair Deal of Harry Truman. Within the Eisenhower context, there is a particular challenge as a new party, as a new generation of governmental managers come to government, taking over a state that had been vastly changed and vastly evolved. To give us perspective and to tell us more about this, it's my pleasure to introduce to you six gentlemen who have played in their own capacities, in all ways, a major role in the modern presidency and who, in the domestic area, have had to confront the issues of big government, enhanced regulatory power, more demands for improved and enhanced services. Let me introduce them to you briefly and then I'll ask each after a more extended introduction to give a four minute or so brief thought to the Eisenhower legacy in domestic affairs. Once we've gone through this panel in that manner, I'll ask our panelists a series of rapid-fire questions and, hopefully, we can get some rapid-fire answers, not only about the Eisenhower legacy but about the functioning of the modern presidency so that, from this rich mixture of service in different administrations, multiple administrations, we can gain an appreciation for the modern presidency.

Let me introduce briefly to you our distinguished panelists. Of course, we're glad to have joining with us again former Attorney General Brownell. Mr. Brownell, it is our pleasure to have you with us. Mr. Rocco Siciliano, Jim Cannon, and, as I move over to my left and to your right, Robert C. Wood, Arthur Flemming and Ralph Bledsoe.

Herbert Brownell doesn't really need a re-introduction to this group but suffice to say that he, of course, brings rich experience in the Eisenhower Administration, a long time lawyer, a partner in the law firm of Lord, Day, and Lord, Barrett, Smith for fifty years. He was Attorney General under the Eisenhower administration. President Reagan appointed him to the Commission on the Bicentennial of the U. S. Constitution. He is a member of numerous national commissions. His experience and role in campaigning, in American politics, and administration go back to the administration of Governor Tom Dewey in New York, and Dewey's campaigns for the Presidency. Attorney General Brownell, could you share with us a few brief thoughts about the Eisenhower legacy in domestic affairs?

Herbert Brownell: I, of course, was in the field of law enforcement and President Eisenhower, during the 1952 Presidential campaign, made one promise, and that was to clean up the mess in Washington. As a matter of fact his opponent, Adlai Stevenson, made the same promise. So you can see that there was something to be done along that line. In the old Department of Justice, when we arrived, one of the assistant attorney generals was especially under fire and we had to clean house before beginning. It turned out that we sent 20 collectors of internal revenue to jail and one of the assistant attorney generals. It was a real mess in the tax collection area especially. It turned out that the reason for that mess was two things: one is that people with axes to grind used to go to the White House when they wanted to get "off the hook" so to speak, from prosecution. The White House would then send them over to the Justice Department and the Justice Department, in those days, took the attitude of "Well, if it comes out of the White House, I guess the President must want me to do this," and they would very often do these favors. It got to be a scandal. The second reason was that one or two of the reporters in Washington had an arrangement with the Attorney General, one of my predecessors, that if there was a criminal investigation underway and it was a "juicy" one, they would leak it to the press, to these reporters. Even though the investigation turned out that the person was innocent, the story would have been told and the reputation of the person would have been irreparably damaged. President Eisenhower recognized that mess in Washington and he made it very clear to all of us at the Justice Department that law enforcement was separate from politics. If anybody claimed to come from the White House and to speak for him on the matter of law enforcement, we were not only to disregard it but we were to repudiate it. I think that was really his legacy in the field of law enforcement, and my staff appreciated that because they could make their own professional decisions as to whether a person should be prosecuted or not, whether an anti-trust case should be carried forward, whether a tax matter should be settled and that was really a great boon to all of us; to have that Presidential leadership which meant "hands off" as far as politics was concerned in the field of law enforcement.

David Kozak: Thank you very much, Mr. Attorney General. As we go on, I think it is important to keep a perspective on the Eisenhower administration with certain emphases and you've really contributed with this emphasis on the notion that, at the presidential level, with presidential leadership, there was an emphasis to keep politics and law enforcement activities separate; that's a very useful and helpful contribution as we try to move through our understanding of Ike's legacy in domestic policy.

I would now like to turn to Mr. Rocco Siciliano, a businessman who served on the White House staff of President Eisenhower as Special Assistant to the President for Personnel Management. He later served as the Deputy Secretary of Commerce under Maurice Stans in the Nixon Administration. He currently lives in Beverly Hills, California, where he served as Chairman of the California Business Roundtable. Mr. Siciliano, what perspective would you like to offer us with regard to Eisenhower's domestic legacy?

Rocco Siciliano: Well, I would like to speak about the point that Attorney General Brownell has made and certainly want to support it. I spent four years as Assistant Secretary of Labor where I was concerned with the nationwide efforts in manpower and employment. I then had the privilege of going over to the White House as Special Assistant to the President in another somewhat closely defined area having to do with manpower involving Federal civilian employees. That was a totally different change. When I left the Labor Department, I was an *operating* officer there, responsible for probably half of the department's activities in employment and manpower. To support the point that Mr. Brownell has made, when I moved to the White House as Special Assistant to the President, I have to carefully say that in those days that was a fairly rarified title. There were only six or eight such special assistants, and you could not use the words "to the President" unless you were a special assistant. Since that time, the numbers have multiplied many, many fold and people do use the title "to the President" quite easily. We were also following an injunction which President Eisenhower himself imposed. The injunction was to follow an earlier recommendation regarding White House staff people; that earlier injunction was that you were supposed to have a "passion for anonymity." That's not my phrase, that's a phrase that was made by the Brownlow Commission of the 1930's when it proposed the "institutional Presidency" for the White House. We had a passion for anonymity; in other words, don't talk and don't try to run the departments. You are here as a staff person, working for the President of the United States and we followed that very, very closely. We did not have press conferences, we did not cater to the press to try to build up our own media kind of impressions. I will say that what has happened since is pretty obvious to the public. With that kind of instruction, I was able to compare the two jobs, the one in operations as a fairly important sub-head of a major cabinet agency and the other working as a staff officer in the White House. Now, who did the domestic policy planning? President Eisenhower, keep in mind, was a military person who was used to knowing what good staff work amounted to. He, himself, had placed first in his class at the Command and General Staff School. He firmly imposed domestic policy planning on the then Bureau of the Budget. The Director of the Bureau of the Budget was the key person responsible for overall domestic policy and planning. Since that time, and I won't get into it further, in subsequent administrations the whole domestic affairs policy planning, including international, has now been moved over into the White House proper.

David Kozak: Thank you very much, Mr. Siciliano. I pick up, I think, two very important notes here for students of the American Presidency. One is that we get a different perspective when you're in an administration out in a department or an agency versus serving within the White House staff; and the second is that we really have seen a great growth in White House staff and in those who have titles of Assistant to the President or Special Assistant. There are, it seems, many more of those folks serving at that level in today's Presidency. But, we also look forward, as we go through our study of the presidency, to getting some of your comments about labor policies and the legacy there.

I would like now to introduce Mr. James Cannon. If you're my age and interested in government and politics, he really doesn't need an introduction for his by-line was always too familiar and always provided lots of insights in both *Time* and *Newsweek* where he wrote for many years. Mr. Cannon, like former Attorney General Brownell, "cut his teeth" in New York politics. He did so with another former governor, Governor Nelson Rockefeller. He came into the Ford administration via the Rockefeller organization where he served as Assistant to the President for Domestic Policy. He has been a director of the Eisenhower Centennial, served as Executive Director of American Agenda, and was a former chief of staff for the former Majority Leader of the United States Senate, Howard Baker. We've asked Jim Cannon to come here and first share some thoughts about the Eisenhower legacy and then later on we'll get into questions on some thoughts and comparisons between Ford and Eisenhower. Mr. Cannon.

James Cannon: Thank you, David. Every White House since Eisenhower has been the beneficiary of the legacy of the Eisenhower staff system.

As Rocco has just said, this system was an outgrowth of his own military experience. The principle, as it is practiced in the White House, is simple to state but not always easy to carry out. The principle is that you subject every good idea, every brilliant proposal, every problem, to some kind of serious analysis with particular emphasis on exposing the idea to its natural enemies before you go public with it. Now, every administration brings in bright men and women with great ideas to save the country and help the President to solve problems. Obviously the President himself comes in with a lot of ideas, a lot of political promises that he would like to bring about; not always good; in fact, very few are good.

How do you separate one good idea from the others. What Eisenhower bequeathed was this process; a process where you considered an idea by an internal debate between those knowledgeable staff people who support the idea and those knowledgeable staff people who are the natural enemies of the idea. This is easier said than accomplished. It must be a tough, rigorous, candid debate and the President must be willing to subject his own ideas to this process. This is organized policy formation and execution and in your book is a quote by Eisenhower himself which says it well: "Its purpose is to simplify, clarify, expedite, and coordinate; it is a bulwark against chaos, confusion, delay, and failure."

In the Ford administration, we took this very seriously. We had inherited the Nixon staff system which was a variation of the Eisenhower staff system and President Ford wanted the issue first defined on paper because he knew that writing disciplines the mind. Writing is another way of thinking. So, in the Domestic Council which I headed, we undertook to collect all the facts; to state the issue as clearly as we could; to describe the merits of the idea and its faults; and then, we sent this paper in with a summary of one, two, three pages. We sent to the President also the more detailed arguments of everyone involved. This would often be a document with a cover of two or three pages and six tabs outlining each Cabinet member's arguments, O.M.B.'s, or whoever had been brought in to the process. Everyone was certain that his ideas, his own arguments, went directly to the President. This Eisenhower system worked for us. It worked well when we did it and when we didn't do it, we had problems. It worked for the problems that land up on the White House doorstep every day; all of us who have been in the White House know that.

To make my point, let me give you just a few examples of presidential decisions that were *not* subjected to this rigorous internal examination and debate. Under Kennedy, the Bay of Pigs. Under Johnson, the expansion of the war in Vietnam. Under Nixon, the Watergate break-in. Under Ford, the WIN program. Under Carter, the failed attempt to rescue the hostages in Iran. Under Reagan, Iran-Contra. Under George Bush, no new taxes. The arguments speak for themselves.

David Kozak: Thank you very much, Jim. Of course, students of the presidency have long been preoccupied with the staff structures of the Eisenhower administration. It really does mark a different kind of presidency with an emphasis on order and routine and regularized processes and I'm glad you mentioned that. As we take our tour through domestic policy, I think it's a very important facet to emphasize.

As we move over to the other side now, I would like to introduce to you Robert C. Wood. Robert C. Wood served as Secretary of Housing and Urban Development in the Johnson Administration. He is a well known and highly published urbanologist. He currently is Henry Luce Professor of Democratic Institutions at Wesleyan. He previously served as superintendent of the Boston public schools and as President of the University of Massachusetts. Those of us who have studied the presidency and who teach the presidency are long indebted to him for his many thoughtful reflections on intergovernmental relations, urban policy and a wonderful piece that he and I were just chatting about that compares the public interest more than twenty years ago called *When Government Works*. Dr. Wood, what can you add to our discussions today? Of course, you had the vantage point of the Johnson years but, is there something you would like to focus on or bring out about the Eisenhower legacy in domestic affairs.

Robert C. Wood: David, in this company and with this distinguished set of colleagues, I feel somewhat like a lion in the den of Daniels. I was a "spear carrier" in the Eisenhower administration and my time, as you suggest, of brief authority, came a decade later. In 1952, I was in the Bureau of the Budget in the Government Organization Branch at a time when Percival Brundage and Fred Lawton were the directors. The whole set of superb civil servants, Elmer Staats, Arnold Miles, Bill Finan, Harold Seidman and Allen Dean were my colleagues and I was a junior person in a very feisty bunch. The Budget Bureau at that time had come "on line" as Jim and the Attorney General have indicated. The success of World War II was behind us. We believed that we had solved the Depression; that we could do almost anything; and that we were capable of understanding America and capable of taking care of the new administration. We were mostly "ivy league," so President Eisenhower's arrival did not especially impress us. We thought of West Point as probably a second rate engineering school and we knew Annapolis was a third rate engineering school. We were worried about a president who seemed to like the country the way it was. There was a period of "arms length" negotiation between these first versions of the "whiz kids," and the new administration as Bob Johnson came in from Temple and as Nelson Rockefeller came in on reorganization. Seidman and Dean and Wood played three dimensional tic tac toe. We wrote memoranda that never went anywhere. The only one that went anywhere was when we pointed out that Staats, who was the then Deputy Director,—his name, spelled backwards, was Staats. We put another in a black book saying, "Why not try cameralism." It got to Sherman Adams before it was detected.

Time went on and the appreciation of the savvy and of the President and of the White House and of the Cabinet grew. I want to simply reinforce the comments of my colleagues before me. The first basic contribution of Eisenhower was to enhance the capacity of the executive office and the President and it was not only a professional in the Budget Bureau that became chief of staff, it was Jim Killian as Presidential Science Advisor, it was the restoration of the Council of Economic Advisors. These steps made it possible to "do" domestic policy. I have spent a good deal of my life trying to follow the two issues in which I think the Eisenhower contributions, domestically, were the greatest; they are urban renewal and the interstate highway program. I say that knowing that on the left and the right, criticism of both these programs have been heavy, but I test an effective policy idea by two standards: 1) did it fit the temper and the needs at the time and 2) does it endure into our present time. Urban renewal was an effort that came about in the time of the great suburban migration in America. The Forty Nine Housing Act had already started it; it was underway. It was to be the greatest migration within the shortest period of time that this country had ever experienced. The question there was: what happened to the cities when they emptied out? What happened to the core city? What happened to the central business district? The Eisenhower 1954 Urban Renewal Program became the first response to put together a remarkable coalition of strong mayors, tough civic leaders and businessmen. It slowed the suburban sprawl and the spread city and it was a vital force in renewing central cities everywhere.

In the interstate highway program one could not conceive of

America prospering in the 1950's without a transportation system that would dramatically reduce overall economic costs. That system moved goods with its 41,000 miles, to tie together this country as a national network. Without it, our economic progress would be inconceivable. One important footnote on that is that President Eisenhower resisted and, at first, rejected moving the interstate highways into central cities. That was the doing of mayors and local business. The comments that had been made incorrectly about the loss of housing of 300,000 urban renewal, 400,000 in interstate highways were not in the original package. We learned, I think, as the '60's and '70's came on. We've built housing as well as commercial development and we empowered, to some extent, the poor people who were in the neighborhoods at that time. We have persevered and we still have a fighting chance for the American cities today. We still have an opportunity to restore some civic and urban culture and I can only hope that in the 1990's we do as well as the Eisenhower people did in the 1950's.

David Kozak: Thank you very much Robert C. Wood. I thank you also for the contribution with regard to substantive public policy. We see with Dr. Woods' remarks an emphasis on two important substantive achievements, urban renewal and the Federal interstate highway system, both of which have to be addressed as we try to develop an understanding for the Eisenhower legacy in domestic policy.

It is now my pleasure to introduce to you Secretary Arthur Flemming, former Secretary of Health, Education and Welfare (HEW, an acronym we've since lost as government has expanded and developed). Secretary Flemming, as an educator, has served in so many different facets of government including the Civil Service Commission and various directorships involving the oversight of the Peace Corps. He has been Chairman of the Civil Rights Commission, a very distinguished career in public service. Secretary Flemming, what can you add to our deliberations this morning and our understanding of Eisenhower and domestic policy?

Arthur Flemming: I'm very, very happy to have the opportunity of doing a little reminiscing with this distinguished panel. My first contact with President Eisenhower was after his election when I was invited to come to New York to become a member of what turned out to be the President's Advisory Committee on Government Organization. He had invited Nelson Rockefeller to chair that particular group. He had invited his brother to be a member of the group and I was invited to be the third member of the group. We held our first meeting prior to the inauguration at Morningside Heights in New York. Preparatory to that meeting, Milton and I had breakfast together and we focused our discussion on the Cabinet. Both of us had been around Washington and we had heard something about Cabinet meetings; by and large they were "show and tell" meetings. We had an idea that the President could use the Cabinet in a little different way. We decided we would bring that up at this meeting with the President-elect, which we did. He said, "Well, I've been thinking along those lines also and everybody tells me that you really can't do very much with the Cabinet as a collegial body under our form of government." The discussion didn't last very long and, at the end, Milton and I decided that we had not made very much progress but I was invited to join the Cabinet as Director of the Office of Defense Mobilization. I was there, of course, at the first meeting of the Cabinet and was very, very interested to hear the President say to the members of the Cabinet, "When you come to a Cabinet meeting, you're not coming just to represent your department or agency, you're coming as a general advisor to me." I was also interested to hear him say, "We're going to have an agenda (that was kind of unheard of prior to that time) and we're going to have staff papers backing up each one of the items on the agenda." He indicated that he was going to read those staff papers and he really expected the rest of us to read them too. Very shortly after that, he indicated that he was going to have a Secretary to the Cabinet, Max Rabb, who is here in the audience and was with us yesterday afternoon. Brad Patterson joined him as his assistant. We were going to have minutes at the end of the meeting; there would be a minute, not a discussion minute, but a minute saying that certain items were discussed and, as a result of those discussions, the President reached a particular decision. I was very, very interested in all of that but I was *particularly* interested in the way in which the President utilized these procedures. In my judgment, he was the *best* practitioner or consulter of management that I've ever seen in action in or out of the government. He would open up a controversial item himself and you would get some indication of where he stood on that particular item; then he would encourage everyone to get into that discussion. He would participate himself but he didn't participate in such a way to shut off discussion but to encourage discussion. After the discussion had gone on for what was sometimes a considerable period of time, he would indicate his conclusion. Sometimes he would say, "Well, I'm not going to 'shoot from the hip' on this one. I'll think about it and you'll get my decision in the minute." I found those discussions to be of tremendous value as a member of the Cabinet. Near the end of his life, I had the opportunity of talking to him alone and he came back to this concept of the Cabinet. He told me that he found these discussions to be of tremendous help to him. Of course, the National Security Council really operated in exactly the same way. I was a member of that during his first term and saw him in action as chair of the National Security Council. So, he set the stage for the introduction of creative ideas; for the consideration of creative ideas. During that first term, for example, I had the opportunity of participating in discussions on the National Defense Education Act and participating in discussions on expanding Social Security to include disability. I didn't feel that it was improper for me to get into it, I was encouraged to get into it. Then, of course, when I was Secretary of Health, Education and Welfare, I knew I could get certain items on the agenda, I could get them before him, I could get a vigorous discussion on it and I could get a decision from him. At the beginning, he said to his then Director of the Budget and of Communication, "I want this administration to be known as an administration that moves forward as far as programs affecting people are concerned." He indicated he didn't want a giant leap forward but he wanted a consistent forward movement; and I think that in one area after another the evidence indicates that it worked and we *did* move forward in a very, very consistent manner. It seems to me that he made a tremendous contribution to the governments of our country by indicating that, "yes, you can, in a very meaningful way, utilize the Cabinet as a collegial body."

David Kozak: Thank you very much, Mr. Secretary. Indeed we are grateful to you for that focus on Cabinet government. For students of the Presidency, the Eisenhower administration is synonymous with Cabinet government, with the use of the Cabinet not only for coordinative purposes but for collective advice and counsel; that is an important part of legacy. We hope, in subsequent discussion here and in other forums at this conference, we'll have an opportunity to develop a better understanding of Eisenhower-style Cabinet government.

It is now my pleasure to introduce to you Ralph Bledsoe. Ralph is currently the Director of the Washington Public Affairs Center for the University of Southern California. Dr. Bledsoe went to work for the Reagan administration at the outset in its early period. He served in a variety of positions within the White House, culminating as the Executive Secretary to the Domestic Policy Council. Dr. Bledsoe has, on other occasions, given very helpful commentaries about relationships between presidential personalities and decision style and management efforts. I would like to ask Dr. Bledsoe, from the vantage point of both academe and for the Reagan years, to comment on the Eisenhower legacy in domestic policy. Ralph.

Ralph Bledsoe: Thank you. I would like to point to two things that I think are of particular importance to presidencies subsequent to the Eisenhower Presidency and that represent his legacy. First, Dr. Flemming has very accurately and forcefully described the executive presidency that President Eisenhower created. This is certainly a vital legacy that was passed on to subsequent presidents. His relationships with the Cabinet, and his insistence on staff work done properly, staff work done in concert with Cabinet members, represents a true contribution from which other presidencies have certainly benefitted. The second legacy I would point to is the stability with which President Eisenhower approached his presidency. I draw on a concept of change which Kurt Lewin coined many years ago. Lewin said, "For change to be successful, it must go through three phases; there must be an 'un-freezing' period, in which an organization or an individual gets ready for change; then there's a change period that occurs; and finally there must be a 're-freezing', or a period of stability for the change that has occurred to take hold and to have an effect." If one looks at World War II as a period of great unfreezing for the country, when we were shaken out of our isolationist thinking, and assume the post war presidency was a period of change, using as an example President Truman's many reorganization plans and formation of so many of the cohort organizations that we now have today, President Eisenhower's presidency can be viewed as providing the stability—the period of time in which those programs were allowed to work and those organizations took effect. This is not to say that he didn't make a lot of changes of his own, but he did it with stability, saying, "Let's keep some things on the right track and let's 'fine tune' others as we move through the post-war period." That was important to us, because the next eight year presidency was that of President Reagan. There were five presidents in between, each of whom left under circumstances I am sure they would not have wanted to leave under. Thus, when we approached the presidency, Eisenhower's legacies were what we tried to look at. We had high hopes that ours would be an eight year presidency, but at the time we didn't know that it would be. In 1982, when we developed the President's Management Improvement Program, we even called it Reform 88, with the idea that we wanted to insert some stability into the management improvement process and to the management of the Federal government, which were two of the areas that I was involved with.

As to the legacy of an executive presidency, Rocco, we had 50 Special Assistants to the President when I was there, 17 or 18 Deputy Assistants, and 8 to 10 Assistants to the President. So, you are absolutely right; the size of the staff has grown. Technically, we had one fewer staff member than the Carter presidency; but if you add the detailees and the volunteers and the others who are around the White House to serve the President, clearly you have a huge growth of staff. But, President Reagan was concerned about the importance of the Cabinet, and did not want the White House staff to encroach on that. I am glad that the domestic policy arena was mentioned. We had seven domestic Cabinet councils in the first term, narrowing those down to two in the second term. This meant that Cabinet members came to the White House a great deal. Domestic policy is an area that presidents don't like to spend too much time on if they can help it, because in that arena are 535 experts on domestic issues at the other end of Pennsylvania Avenue, and as Brad Patterson pointed out, some 17,000 to 18,000 special interest groups in this country, each of which is expert in some aspect of domestic policy (that's probably why we have twelve domestic Cabinet departments and only two in the national security arena). Domestic policy making has certainly changed and I think that President Eisenhower was the one who set the tone by having a broad agenda; and by delegating it to the staff and to the Cabinet members to try to make it work. We certainly tried to follow these legacies.

David Kozak: Thank you very much, particularly for the focus on the use of staff, on attentive and dutiful staff work, and also on the necessity for stability. The presidency is a provider of not only national unity but national stability. In many ways, the history of the '60's and '70's were shaped by a series of one term presidencies; that kind of rotating succession of leadership did cause problems of instability in domestic programming and planning.

I think we're indebted to this panel for six very different vantage points on the domestic legacy of the Eisenhower administration. First, we get an emphasis on a genuine effort to keep the enforcement of the law above politics; certainly good advice for any future administration. We get an emphasis on the necessity for anonymity among White House staffers if there is to be effective staff action of operations within the White House. We get an emphasis on the internal processes of debate and deliberation and development of options. We get an emphasis on substantive policy areas that have borne much fruit but also have been very challenging to the Nation's cities. We get an emphasis on Cabinet government and, in conclusion, we received an emphasis on staff and stability. Each offering a different vantage point but also a core concept that students of the Eisenhower presidency are obliged to use when trying to understand not only the Eisenhower presidency but the modern presidency.

I have a series of questions that I would like to throw out to our panelists. Maybe we can get their rapid-fire response so we get through some of them. Then we can turn to the folks in the audience for some questions that this richly blended panel can respond to. I think all who work in the realm of domestic policy, all who study it, all who think about it, would agree with so many practitioners when they say, "A challenge of the American presidency is that we have a government of sub-governments." The way we develop and implement most of our domestic programs and policies is frequently with a narrow agency parochial view or perspective. What the vexing problems of the day require is a much more comprehensive view point. The difficulty is generating some type of comprehensiveness in government.

A question I would throw out to our panelists is: in the Eisenhower years, particularly for those who served in the Eisenhower years, what was done to coordinate our government of sub-governments; to make it a little more effective, a little more comprehensive. If you were not in the Eisenhower years, what has been done since that time which has been effective in addressing that challenge. Why don't we start with our former Attorney General. Mr. Attorney General, would you like to comment at all on coordinating the government of sub-governments?

Herbert Brownell: I might tell a personal experience that I had during the Eisenhower years. The President asked me to sit in on the National Security Council meeting and it was there that I learned his methods of contingency planning. He always said to us, "Now you've got to be prepared for the emergencies; maybe the contingency planning won't work out the way you thought; but getting acquainted and cooperating with the people that you'll have to work with in an emergency is very valuable in itself." Now, I'll tell you how that affected me.

You will remember in those days, everybody was afraid that the atomic bomb was going to be dropped on us in the United States. We had elaborate contingency plans as to what would happen if Washington, D.C. was wiped out. Each one of the Cabinet officials was sent on a given day to a hideout in the Catoctin Mountains where we were supposed to carry on skeleton duties when the atomic bomb dropped over Washington. The Justice Department was sent out to Martinsburg, West Virginia, and we were told that, in case of an emergency, the President would have to operate from the underground. The Pentagon would have to turn to us for advice on keeping national emergency problems within the Constitution. I drilled my team quite extensively and this was my first great experience in carrying out my contingency planning. They told us bulletins would come from time to time as to what was happening throughout the United States in this great national emergency. Well, the first bulletin came out and it read, "The Attorney General and his staff have just been wiped out by a bomb." Eisenhower was right—you didn't always carry out exactly what you planned in the way of contingency planning. I never had the opportunity to ask President Eisenhower whether he personally drafted that first bulletin wiping out the Attorney General.

Arthur Flemming: I had the responsibility of developing those plans as Director of Defense Mobilization. I didn't put that particular line in but I remember presenting the overall plan to President Eisenhower one day. He looked at it and said, "It reads okay, but it isn't worth the paper it's written on unless we test it." He said, "We're going to have an annual test on this. Your colleagues in the Cabinet won't be very happy about it but *I'm* going to participate and *they* will participate;" and he did participate.

Rocco Siciliano: I would like to add to that. The Secretary of Labor was also eliminated and I was told that I was to relocate the War Manpower Administration of which I would be the War Manpower Administrator, to Chambersburg, Pennsylvania, which we did. Several hundred of us moved up to Chambersburg for a period of days and took over a college. For three years in a row—two years in Chambersburg and one in Virginia (for other reasons, we didn't go back to Virginia because they had, at that time, been practicing segregation and we moved to Pennsylvania)—I was the War Manpower Administrator. The fact is that you had to leave your wife and family, and take off for four or five days. We did this, and my wife, who is sitting in the front row, kept saying, "What about us? What happens to us?" The fact is, I assume you were to be sacrificed.

Robert Wood: Jim, on the issue of stability and organization, it's awfully important to remind ourselves that Eisenhower came out of the organized, large institutional world. He was followed by Kennedy and by Johnson who were legislators and their whole approach, unfamiliar with large organizations, not committed as much to coordination as to bartering and brokering, made the White House, in different circumstances, quite a different place. I think the experience of the '50's, even though from the outside there was a notion that maybe it was too calm, was one that has not been replicated since that time.

Arthur Flemming: On the question of coordination, I feel that Eisenhower's approach to the Cabinet *did* promote coordination. Incidentally, I don't personally react favorably to describing it as Cabinet Government. That implies that the Cabinet was governing overall. It seems to me that what he did was to develop an approach utilizing the Cabinet as a collegial body in providing him with advice and consultation on the issues. In a way, he *was* coordinating the advice that he would get from his Cabinet by utilizing the Cabinet meeting in this way and by tying that in with the staff support that he provided at the White House.

I also think that we do need to keep in mind the fact that the first assignment that he gave this Advisory Committee on Government Organization was to carry out the pledge that he made during his campaign to create a department in the welfare area. After all, up to that time all of those programs had not been represented at the Cabinet table. Many of them were in the Federal Security Agency but the head of that was not at the Cabinet table. That was the first assignment he gave us and we were able to come up with a reorganization plan utilizing the management staff of the Bureau of the Budget. We did not set up a staff of our own; we had one staff director, we utilized the people that Secretary Wood has described and they rendered this very effective service. As a result, we had our reorganization plan in effect by April, 1953, which was very fast work. That, in and of itself, was a coordinating device to try to bring together all of those programs affecting people and providing some effective coordination in those areas.

Rocco Siciliano: I want to follow up on the point that Arthur Flemming has made with respect to the Advisory Committee on Government Organization. One of the recommendations made to the President, which he did adopt, was to create by Executive Order, the job to which I was appointed, the Special Assistant to the President for Personnel Management. This was not a patronage type of job; in fact, explicitly set forth in the Executive Order was the requirement that the incumbent of that job have nothing to do with patronage or political appointments. It consisted entirely of something that the general American public was basically totally unaware of, and yet was so needed; that is, within the public service, over 2,100,000 Americans were employed by the Federal government. There are roughly 1,000 different occupations. At that time, there were over 60 separate compensation systems; everybody just says the "civil service" or the "public service," being quite unaware that we have different systems throughout all of the government: the Bureau of Medicine and Surgery, the Foreign Service Act, and it just goes on and on and on. The President felt that there should be some kind of coordination and recognition of all of these different systems which exist in the Federal service; so he created the job that I was appointed to. It was a staff job but, at the same time, you had to work very closely with the Secretary of Defense, with the Secretary of HEW, and so on. It was the first position in the White House to have a staff of its own other than National Security. It was the beginning of the later systems that followed with successive presidents. Unfortunately, a succeeding President, President Kennedy, thought about it and decided to abolish that role; but many years later, there was created the Office of Personnel Management.

Ralph Bledsoe: Just a couple of thoughts on that. One is that President Reagan instituted a management improvement effort that looked at the entire government. Reform 88 was intended to be an umbrella under which Federal organizations could begin to examine the cross-cutting management and administrative areas where we could save funds, such as reducing the number of payroll/personnel systems, or the numbers of accounting systems. We tried to "crosswalk" data from organization to organization. I think that this reform, begun by President Eisenhower was followed through during the Reagan administration.

My other thought has to do with the "situation" in which

our two colleagues were "sacrificed," I guess that's the way it was put earlier. President Eisenhower was the last president to personally participate in one of those emergency contingency planning efforts. In the Reagan administration, we were concerned about the crisis response capability within the White House enough that the Vice President was placed in charge of the development of an improved crisis management process. I am happy to say it is much better today than it was when we arrived.

James Cannon: I just want to add one point to the point added a minute ago about Eisenhower having run his organization and about his immediate successors having been legislators. I was a journalist at that time, and during several subsequent presidencies, and it was my observation then, and still is, that there is a profound difference between a President who comes from having run something and a President who has come from the legislative process. Basically it is: generally speaking, a good president or a governor for the most part, had to make up his mind at the start of the process, and then persuade others, the legislature, the Cabinet, the public, to follow along with his program. The legislator in Washington, by definition, tends to make up his mind at the end of the process, that is when they vote—when all the arguments have been made. There is a different cast of mind. In my view, it is important to note that one of the most important things about a successful President is that he know how the Federal government works; and Eisenhower obviously did. He had spent enough time in Washington. There are no politics more energetic than Pentagon politics. He knew how Washington worked. He had been up on the Hill many, many times. He knew how the place worked. Johnson knew how Washington worked and that was one of the reasons that he could be such an effective president. Ford knew how the government worked but had other problems, having inherited some problems from Nixon, and he was not successful. My own feeling about Carter and, to some extent, President Reagan, was that they came to Washington *not* with a clear understanding of how Washington worked, to the extent that they did *not* understand it, and they had great problems.

Arthur Flemming: On your observation between the governors or people who have had executive experience and the legislators, President Eisenhower, to some extent, was the exception to that. He did make up his mind at times after listening to a very vigorous discussion. I can cite at least one instance where, from my point of view, if I had received a decision from him before the Cabinet discussion, it would have been a negative decision. As a result of vigorous Cabinet debate and discussion, it became a positive decision. He did listen. He participated. As a result of that participation in the discussion process, at times his position would shift.

James Cannon: I was thinking more of the Eisenhower who created the interstate highway system which I consider one of the most profound decisions made at this time and he made it on his own, for good reasons; out of his own experience, out of his military experience, out of his foresight to see a commercial need in the country, and it has obviously had a profound effect. He put it through the Congress over the most extraordinary opposition from railroads and shippers and a whole lot of other people.

Robert Wood: I might add that the legislative or Congressional style then, and still now, is the disposition of a Senator or a Congressman to pick a single issue or two, and become an expert on it; that makes it very difficult. One of the extraordinary things about Lyndon Johnson was his capacity to get beyond that. It was very difficult for them [legislators] to set priorities or coordinate among themselves. I think, even as the Eisenhower period seemed to be stable or at times not exciting, that capacity of rank-ordering priorities stands out as a major characteristic.

Rocco Siciliano: I haven't been asked, but I would like to make a comparison between the six and a half years that I spent in the Eisenhower administration and some ten years later when I was asked to be the Number Two man in the U.S. Department of Commerce, a position that is now called Deputy Secretary to Commerce. I spent roughly two years in that administration under President Nixon and I saw an enormous difference going back to process and staff operations. We not only had all of the huge numbers of special assistants and deputy assistants to the president, people who in the Eisenhower years might have been called a staff assistant *period,* but who are now Assistants to the President. The focus had shifted from the Bureau of the Budget to what is now called the Office of Management and Budget and went even beyond that to the creation, within the White House proper (now that shouldn't be taken literally because there aren't that many offices in the White House proper, they are over in the Old State Building which is right across the street, but, nevertheless, that's what it was called, the White House proper). I found confusion and a multiplicity of authorities as the Number Two man in charge of General Management of the Department of Commerce, which is a conglomerate of some forty or more thousand employees. It, too, has a range of activities from the Bureau of Standards to the Patent Office to International Trade and so on; it was a totally different picture ten years later and I thought nostalgically of those days when there was a tight knit control—you knew who to go to, and my people within the Commerce Department were getting telephone calls from innumerable staffers in the White House at various levels; whereas, in the Eisenhower years, you weren't allowed to call people, three or four or five levels down, you dealt only with the peer person; that is, the Secretary or the Undersecretary. It's quite a difference. That, by the way, is pretty much the way it is, not just under the Nixon years but even more so as other presidents came in. I don't mean this as a political thing.

David Kozak: Why don't we shift gears a little bit and talk about multiple advocacy. It's a shame that Roger Porter is not here with us this morning. He has not been able to get free from Washington because of all the wrangling about the budget and the deficit. I think students of the American Presidency are in general agreement, and Jim Cannon alluded to this before, that you make good policy through what's called multiple advocacy; that is, having a lot of different viewpoints coming to bear on a particular question, lots of vigorous debate and, when a decision is made, the decision-maker, the President, has the advantage of lots of different vantage points; a wide spectrum of advice and information and input.

Now, a question I think I would like to ask both of those who served in the Eisenhower administration and those who have served subsequent administrations is this: did the formal structure of the Eisenhower administration highly formalize the chain of command; an emphasis on doing business in a stable regularized way, the use of the Cabinet, the use of the staff, the use of the NSC staff: did that facilitate multiple advocacy; did it bring a lot of positions to bear or were there some difficulties, particularly when you had a strong chief of staff and the presence of Governor Sherman Adams? Was that a liability, having a strong man as chief of staff in having this kind of multiple advocacy process? Why don't we start off with Attorney General Brownell and try to go through our panelists very quickly with regard to the decision process.

Herbert Brownell: To illustrate the problem that you present, I would say that my outstanding experience was in connection with the Civil Rights Act of 1957. In that case, I realized how much autonomy Eisenhower gave to his Cabinet members to develop their own program. We presented the civil rights program to the President first and he said, "Well, this involves matters of high policy which are extremely controversial. I think you should present it directly to the Cabinet." I presented it to the Cabinet and the Cabinet was seriously divided. Some were mildly opposed to the voting rights aspect of the bill. When he saw that division of opinion, he said, "I'll tell you what you do. You present this to Congress as a project of the Justice Department from the Attorney General and *not* as an administration measure," which we did. We not only had the benefit of the thorough Cabinet discussions but we had the benefit from the hearings under the auspices of the Judiciary Committee in the House of Representatives. We really canvassed every aspect of it. The Bill, in that session of Congress, was defeated by filibuster. Then the 1956 Presidential campaign came along and Eisenhower understood all the conflicting views that there were on it and he decided to support the Bill. He advocated the Bill as part of his campaign for re-election in 1956. The point I would like to make is to show how thoroughly he wanted these controversial issues explored before he presented the solution as a product of the Eisenhower administration officially.

David Kozak: Mr. Attorney General, I wanted to ask a

quick follow-up question to you. Did the "strong man chief of staff" structure get in the way of that or were you still able to get a good vigorous debate of policy alternatives?

Herbert Brownell: Whenever we needed to go directly to the President, we were not only authorized to do so but felt free to do so. In my experience at least, I think having a strong chief of staff in the White House was helpful. In that way, we were able to quickly draw out the opinions of other branches and departments of the government.

Arthur Flemming: Sherm Adams saw himself as a facilitator of relationships between the Cabinet and the President. I can give you one instance. When I was Director of Defense Mobilization, I needed some guidance on a policy issue. I thought that Sherm undoubtedly understood what the President's position was on it. I went in to talk to him about it and he said, "Yes, I think I know what his position is, but you should hear it directly from the President. Let's go in and talk with him." We went in and talked and it *was* the same as Sherm Adams thought but he would not step in between the Cabinet officer and the President. My recollection is that Tom Stevens' instructions were, if a Cabinet officer wants to see the President, he's to get on the schedule within 48 hours, if the President was in town.

Rocco Siciliano: I would like to support that. I think a strong chief of staff is essential, regardless of who the President is. The question that you should ask is about the person himself. In Sherman Adams' case he was very selfless, he was brilliant and he was certainly a facilitator. It is with some degree of amusement that I read recently, in a Pulitzer Prize winning book, that Sherman Adams opposed the concept of a meeting with the President and black leaders, particularly the makeup of the group. I happened to be responsible for that (as we have discussed in an earlier session) and it just isn't so, it's absurd. Sherman Adams agreed with the recommendation which we made to him that Martin Luther King, Jr. and A. Philip Randolph, Lester B. Granger and Roy Wilkins would be the group. To read this in a book by a historian, which is otherwise a very good book—it got the Pulitzer Prize—I don't know where it came from because Sherman Adams was no obstacle at all.

James Cannon: There is no question in my mind either that the White House will not work without a good, strong chief of staff. There must be someone there to assist the President in handling the myriad details, the issues and, importantly, the egos. Not everybody gets to see the President right away, not everybody *needs* to see the President right away and a good chief of staff has got to be a "traffic cop," as much as anything else; perhaps a "facilitator" is a better word. We had excellent chiefs in the Ford administration. The first was Don Rumsfeld, he was an honest broker; we had Dick Cheney after that who was also an honest broker. You could see them and, if you needed to see the President, you got to see him, usually in less than 48 hours; but you did not go in with a lone idea and whisper in the President's ear that this is a great thing that we can do. That didn't work. It had to be subjected to this multiple examination of staff people. What the chief of staff did was make sure that the process was fair, that it worked, that everybody who needed to know did know, and had a chance to get the President's ear on the matter.

Ralph Bledsoe: We had two different structures in the Reagan White House from the first term to the second term. In the first term, you may recall, there was a Triad, and sometimes a Quadriad, in charge. We had a chief of staff you could say was a weak chief of staff, because he did not have Cabinet rank, and a Counselor to the President who had Cabinet rank. The Chief of Staff position was a weak one, but not the person in it, Jim Baker. Baker was a very strong chief of staff, but his power was shared with two or three other people in terms of the allocation of staff responsibilities within the White House. Those of us at different levels reported up through one of these four "channels."

One way to divide up the President's responsibilities is to separate his leadership responsibilities and his policy-making responsibilities. Some wonder how President Eisenhower's leadership might work in the White House of today. I think it would not be out of place at all. I think that he would whip the staff into shape first of all, since he was used to a staff that could handle the multiple tasks of a military staff, e.g. G-1, G-2. I don't think he would be unfamiliar with that leadership approach; nor would he be unfamiliar, of course, with a strong chief of staff system.

On the policy side of the White House staff, we had a National Security Advisor and a Counselor to the President who handled foreign policy and domestic policy, respectively. However, they worked closely together. President Eisenhower would have encouraged, and even demanded, that.

In the second Reagan term, we moved to a strong chief of staff model. But, we had three very different chiefs of staff in those positions. You can argue about a strong chief of staff, but it's the behavior of the person in the job—how they facilitate and work to support the President, how they work with the Cabinet, and work with others on the White House staff that makes the difference.

Robert Wood: I think that you would have to add one other dimension otherwise our consensus on staffing can get disturbing and that's really "the context of the times." If you ask in what circumstances diverse views are tolerated, when people are able to put up different ideas, one has to remember that the '50's were reasonably a time of contentment in this nation; and one has to remember that the veterans had come home, we had won the war, depression did not occur contrary to most of the economists of that time and there was a quiet generation in the colleges at that point. Bubbling up discontent and different views were not what they were to become in the '60's. The second point to make is that the data that would have let us know in the '50's, that there were troubles ahead in the '60's, i.e. the migration of 1.6 African-Americans from the tenancy in the south to the slums of the big cities simply didn't become apparent until the 1960's. So, in that sense, a staff organization of the White House presidency operates under different periods of pressure. I think what Eisenhower was able to do was to anticipate, find a breathing spell and use lead time. But it was nothing like being in Lyndon Johnson's administration in 1967, when the cities blew. It was nothing like having to deal with a whole set of new constituencies. The Johnson administration undertook to have a pyramid more than a hub. It certainly was not as relaxed as the Kennedy administration was but I think that the important point is that it make a measure of the pressure that falls on a White House and an organization. Then, the behavior of the chief of staff becomes critical and it's at that point that you begin to see the difference between your people with Ford and the people who had preceded with Johnson. *(Said to James Cannon):* Joe Califano was never a part, as I remember, of your administration.

Arthur Flemming: I think it's important to think of all of this in relationship to the budget process because that's obvious from what's going on at the present time. As a result of President Eisenhower's approach to the Cabinet, and as a result of his staff setup, I felt that we had a very good relationship with him as Cabinet members on the budget. In the first place, the Budget Director was in the Cabinet. He participated in and listened to all of these discussions. In the second place, if we got a markup from the budget that we felt was in conflict with some of the objectives that the President had in mind, we could appeal over at the Budget Bureau level and it was understood that we could appeal, if we felt we needed to, directly to the President.

Take the National Defense Education Act. That was landmark legislation. That was the first time since the Land Grant College Act that the Federal government had gotten into the area of post secondary education. That was passed just as I took office as Secretary of HEW; then we had the problem of getting money to implement it. It was great legislation but it wouldn't have amounted to very much unless we could get some money and everybody was "plowing new ground" on that. It resulted in some pretty vigorous discussion as to how much money was going to be appropriated. Because of the climate the President set, we could appeal and finally got some pretty good decisions that we were able to move forward in the implementation. I think that everything that we have been saying here does have its impact on the budget process and that budget process is terribly important in terms of achieving domestic objectives.

David Kozak: Well, I think that everybody wishes that there wasn't a clock this morning but there *is* one and, regrettably, we're going to have to come to a conclusion here. I just want to say that I think the value of this panel has been not only to emphasize the Eisenhower legacy but also to show us, very richly, the important connection between the times, the political climate of a presidency, but also the structures of a White House, the President's personality, the use of the apparat, and how decisions are made.

CHAPTER FIVE

Eisenhower at Gettysburg

D r. William Ewald served as a special assistant to President Eisenhower in the White House. When the President left office in 1961, he retired to his farm in Gettysburg, Pennsylvania. Dr. Ewald was asked to work at Gettysburg with the President on his memoirs. As a result of this unique relationship, Dr. Ewald provides numerous insights on the Eisenhower presidency and the President himself. Dr. Ewald points out that President Eisenhower was very cognizant of the view that he had a "do nothing" presidency and that he was "out on the golf" course when decisions were made. One of purposes of writing his memoirs, which were started within weeks after the inauguration of John F. Kennedy, was to discuss the issues which faced the administration and how he handled them.

During this session Dr. Ewald vividly describes the process of writing the two volume memoirs, which were done on the campus of Gettysburg College. President Eisenhower had clearly established the agenda for the book and what the chapters would be, starting in 1952 with the election. The drafts of each chapter were joint ventures between the President, Dr. Ewald, and John Eisenhower, the President's son, who became a regular part of the memoir writing team. Throughout Dr. Ewald's discussion, he chronicles often comical issues that President Eisenhower left out of his memoirs but which came up during the writing process.

Such is the case of Alaska's statehood. When President Eisenhower appointed Fred Seaton as Secretary of Interior in his second term, he did not know that Mr. Seaton was committed to the idea of statehood for Alaska. Secretary Seaton passionately pursued the President for statehood for Alaska, and put the President in the uncomfortable position of supporting statehood for a state he felt was "for the birds". Eisenhower ended up supporting statehood rather than go against a cabinet member, but was rewarded by overwhelming public support for the move. In addition, Alaska consistently voted Republican, another bonus for the President.

Dr. Ewald also notes in his discussion President Eisenhower's command of details. Without using any documents, President Eisenhower could easily refer to exact dates, quote national security records, and even quote his own daily diaries. In writing his memoirs, President Eisenhower easily recalled specific details of meetings with members of his Cabinet and staff and members of Congress. Not only were days and times recalled, but the specific conversations involved.

However as Dr. Ewald also notes, President Eisenhower was not perfect in his recollections. In drafting the chapter on the Open Skies proposal to the Russians in 1955, President Eisenhower neglected to include the significant influence of Nelson Rockefeller.

Rockefeller and a brain trust he established had, in fact, conceived the Open Skies concept. However, when Ewald brought this omission to President Eisenhower's attention, it was immediately included in the memoirs.

Dr. Ewald provides a rare view of the personal Eisenhower, his warmth, his charm, his concern for others. It is also an insider's look at the White House of Dwight Eisenhower.

SPEAKER: William Bragg Ewald, Jr.
Assistant on the Eisenhower White House
Staff and Presidential Memoirs, 1954-65

I'd like to talk today about Gettysburg, about Eisenhower in Gettysburg, and about the making of history. "Eisenhower Revisionism," which is a term that really has become applied to historical writing about President Eisenhower in recent years, describes the change in his historical attitude toward his presidency. Eisenhower Revisionism begins in Gettysburg. The first revisionist was Dwight Eisenhower himself. He began writing his two volume memoirs, "White House Years," within weeks after he left Washington and the presidency. He had in his possession all his own personal papers, which have become known now as the Whitman Files, the most intimate, personal treasures, really, of his presidency. He had them all here, right here on the campus of Gettysburg College. He had all his personal recollections, known only to him, of his eight years in the White House and, last but not least, he had his son, John, and me helping him. And I must say that that association, I'm sure for John and certainly for me, was one that we all look back on with great, great affection and warmth.

Now, when you talk about Revisionism, there is no question that Eisenhower had historical adversity to contend with. In January 1961, he was succeeded by a man who had already proved himself as a historian with the book, *Profiles in Courage*, John Kennedy. John Kennedy had on his staff the godfather, in a sense, of the cyclical theory of the presidency, Arthur M. Schlesinger, Jr. Schlesinger was an ardent Democrat, a very, very brilliant writer, and a militantly liberal historian. They came to work in January 1961, convinced that the Schlesinger cyclical theory was about to be re-born under John Kennedy. Now you know how the cyclical theory goes. The cyclical theory holds that we have a succession of presidents. You get an activist, a good guy, a man like Abraham Lincoln, a man like Teddy Roosevelt, a man like Woodrow Wilson. They are people who want to stretch the demands and power of the presidency to their limits. Sometimes they prefer to stretch beyond their limits and really get things in motion—be as big men as they can be. These are the good guys and the activists. After they hold office for a period of time, perhaps eight years, or in the case of Roosevelt and Truman, for twenty years, the country wants a breathing space. So what does it do? It elects a bunch of dullards, or a dullard, such as Warren Harding, Calvin Coolidge, or Herbert Hoover, just to give the country time to digest all this wonderful progress that had been made under the activist preceding him.

Well, here comes 1961. After twenty years of Roosevelt and Truman, eight years of Eisenhower's dullsville presidency and do nothing government gave the country time to digest it all. Now the Administration wants to, in the words of the new president, get America moving again. So these people arrived in Washington, all ready to get America moving again; and, as one of their admirers, Alfred Kazin, once said, "They arrived in Washington and began writing history before they'd made any." They really believed that the activism theory was something that they were going to put into effect. I think you probably remember the early days of John Kennedy. He was not a man who was going to be bound by the staff system—the cumbersome checks and balances and delegations of Eisenhower. He was going to get himself right in touch with the people as a whole. So, what did he do? He began crossing West Executive Avenue, going into the mail room, opening up the sacks of mail with his bare hands, seizing letters right from the individual man on the street and reading them. This would make great theater and great reporting for awhile, but you can't keep that up for very long as President. Pretty soon, he let other people open the mail and read the letters. But this myth really continued. In 1962, Arthur Schlesinger's father came out with a poll that ranked the Presidents. It showed at the top obviously, Washington, Lincoln and Franklin Roosevelt; and way down among the pits below Herbert Hoover, or thereabouts, was Dwight Eisenhower. Eisenhower had been ranked very low in a nationwide poll of historians who I think were working on a cyclical theory.

The brilliant historian Samuel Eliot Morrison of Harvard, a man of very, very keen intellect and rigorous scholarship, wrote "The Oxford History of the American People." It's a brilliant book *until* it gets up to Eisenhower. When he gets to Eisenhower and

Kennedy, he goes absolutely ga ga. It is slipshod, worthless, opinionated, wrong-headed, foolish scholarship. And he's as bad against Eisenhower as he was ga ga over Camelot and John Kennedy. But that just goes to show you how historians can become partisans. We would not deny that this little group we had in Gettysburg, the President, John and I, were partisans also, and we realized very much that we were up against it, with all the media and historical attention being focused on the cyclical theory and the deficiencies of Eisenhower. John Eisenhower at one point said he thought we had one single purpose for those two big volumes that we wrote which covered the first and second terms, as Rusty Brown, who's here in the audience knows, in great detail. The purpose of the two volumes, was simply to show that, in John's words, "Dad knew what was going on. He was not out on the golf course all the time." He knew where Lebanon was and he knew where Suez was, and he knew what was going on up on the Hill, and he was basically a man who understood government. Now that is a very low purpose and a very modest purpose. But, at that time, we thought if we could do that, we at least would have done something. You may notice in the Eisenhower memoirs, there are photographs of Eisenhower's speech drafts and message drafts to the Congress that show typescript, and it's all scribbled up in Eisenhower's own handwriting, simply to show that when he got into something, he really got into it and worked very hard and personally. And so that was one purpose.

Another result of this feeling that we had that we were running uphill and having to work against the historical trend at the time, was in the fact that the two volumes in places acquire a kind of defensive tone. That is, they justify what was done, and I will take a lot of responsibility for that. I thought it was high time we told the truth and let the record speak for itself, all that kind of thing, but I think there is a defensiveness that was inescapable given the times in which we were living.

We worked here on the campus of Gettysburg College at 300 Carlisle Street. The President worked upstairs in a small office, which he liked, and John and I worked downstairs. We had the Whitman files out on that glassed-in porch, which you can see to this day, and we'd pad back and forth, working and consulting the files. I also spent a lot of time in the Library of Congress, because the record of the President cannot depend strictly on his own personal papers; that is, they will tell you part of the story and all of a sudden the story will break off and you have to get to the public record. Also, it cannot depend strictly on the President's recollection, because, as you well know, your memory fails you from time to time. It fails all of us, and certainly much of what we had to do was to get to the documents and records, and establish as well as we could, what the truth was.

But, I will say that it was fun all the way in that group that we had. It's really one of the great joys in my life and I trust that it's still one of the joys of John's life. It was a lot of hard work but it was splendid. Part of the joy of it was John's own sense of humor. John sometimes comes across as a person a bit reserved and a bit modest, but he has one of the best senses of humor of any human being I've ever met. He could see funny things in circumstances that were too subtle for many people to see. For example, President Eisenhower admired Secretary of State John Foster Dulles enormously and he would quote Dulles. He would say, "You know, Foster used to say that we made the finest team in foreign relations, one of the finest teams this country has ever had." He [Dulles] said Eisenhower, after all, had traveled all over the world, knew everybody, conversed with world leaders and knew them intimately and personally—and that's a great thing. And Dulles said, he, himself had studied this field of foreign affairs since he was a child, since 1905, before World War I, and they made a great team. Well, the President always liked to quote that, and he thought that was a fine tribute to him and Foster. John heard that tribute, and the light went on and he said, "Now the way you ought to look at that is that Foster Dulles said, 'With my brains and your contacts, we can't miss.'" Again and again I found that John had really impeccable judgment on what was the fair way to do things, the honest and honorable way. We'd work away here on the text and then we would have a group of our friends from Doubleday and Company, Sam Vaughan and Ken McCormick, come down periodically to see what we were up to and to edit. Sam and Ken were a bit more liberal than John and I were, so they made a very good balance. They would ask a lot of questions, a lot of tough questions, and they would force us to justify our position. I think it was useful and constructive to have that kind of association, because they would keep us on our toes. We would stand up for what we thought was right and modify what we had to modify. They were a valuable part of the operation.

How did we work? Ordinarily we'd do drafts of individual chapters. We knew pretty well what the chapters had to be, starting in 1952, with the election campaign, going all the way to 1961, to the end of the administration. Sometimes the President would do a draft. This was relatively rare. He did drafts of the early chapters, and he did some drafts along the way. He did drafts towards the end of the book because these were places where he had the most personal input and the greatest personal memory of things to say. But in between, once you got into knotty questions of legislation, how the Senate voted, how the House voted, how the compromises worked out, or once we got into details of great foreign problems, that was hard, slogging work. John would do a draft of those chapters and I did a lot of the drafts for those chapters; but then, we all went to work on whatever we had done individually and we'd work things over, take things out, change things and so on.

The President himself was far from being a man who's out on the golf course all the time. I think Rusty Brown, who was his secretary at the time, will tell you, if you look at his handwriting on a page, it's small, it's tiny, it's impeccable; he had huge hands. But handwriting with a sharp pencil, he did not make mistakes and he did not lack clarity and he was always trying to get the thing absolutely right, and it was legible and it was superb editing—editing toward factual accuracy, more than toward sounding good. He was a stickler for grammar. There is a sentence in the first volume that says that a particular controversy that he had, "was the sharpest difference that had ever existed between my staff and I." That's grammatically wrong as any grammarian knows and Eisenhower did not write that "I" in there. I didn't write it in and John didn't write it in, let's leave it at that. It was written in by an editor and it went in at the very last minute and slipped through the net and Eisenhower said, "I never use that expression! I know it's between my staff and me." The trouble with the expression was that it was right in the middle of a sensitive chapter about Joe McCarthy, and so all the newspaper people and everybody jumped on it and said, "Oh, here's Dwight Eisenhower, he doesn't know grammar." Well, he knew enough grammar not to have made that mistake.

When you think of Eisenhower at work, I can't give you a better example than this. You know, he would go out in the winter time to his place in Palm Desert and John and I would go out at times and work with him out there. Mrs. Eisenhower apparently did not like to fly; so they would come back by train from Palm Desert, California, to Gettysburg, Pennsylvania. They had a special railroad car and it took about five days to cross the country. In typical publisher fashion, they sent Eisenhower galleys of his second volume in California and they said, "Dear Mr. President, here are the galley proofs of your second volume. We need them back at the publishing house so the printers can start working by next Monday." Well, Eisenhower and Mrs. Eisenhower were getting on the train and he rode all the way across the country with the train jiggling, the galleys spread out on a table in front of him, making additions and changes and emendations. When he arrived in Gettysburg for sessions that we had, he had a big wad of Kleenex stuffed back behind one of his eyeglasses. His eyes were watering from this awful ordeal. I couldn't have done it but he, at the age of 73 or 74, whatever it was, had done it. He felt that was what he had to do. It demonstrates his sense of responsibility and his sense of accuracy and also his modesty; I mean, an ex-President of the United States has the right to tell a publisher, "Go drop dead. When I get to Gettysburg, I'll do my editing and, if you don't like it, we'll get another publisher." But he didn't do that. He stayed right on schedule and did his editing.

Now, when people ask about Eisenhower's historical judgment on various people or various events, (and people have been calling, asking what did he really think of Mr. Justice Brennan, what did he think of Earl Warren and all this kind of thing), there were certain people that Eisenhower felt rather negative about. At times, he would express negative opinions about Warren; not, I repeat not, about the Supreme Court desegregation decision but he did have reservations about some of the Warren judgments. He had great reservations about Field Marshal Montgomery. I remember after Eisenhower's landslide victory in 1956, Montgomery wrote him a cable that said simply, "Hurrah, hurrah, hurrah." Well, I thought that was great and I put it in the book. Eisenhower struck it out. He said, "I don't want anything in here from Field Marshal Montgomery." And it never got in there. He might refer to a famous foreign statesman as a great drunk but not one breath of that would creep into the manuscript. He might refer to a distinguished United States Senator as a whoremonger off camera, privately, but believe me, that never got in either, even though it was well known to everybody in Washington. So, there were certain things that he muted in his historical judgment. There were also certain things where I would say he turned up the temperature a bit; for example, when we got down to the very end of the second volume, it occurred to me, and I'd been one of the worst offenders on being political and partisan and mean, that there was nothing nice in either volume about either John Kennedy or Lyndon Johnson. I thought it was bad to go out with just nothing; we'd said plenty of negative things about their conduct, particularly Johnson's and what he'd done. It just looked unbalanced, and Eisenhower agreed; so he said, "Well, fine," and he went away and dictated to Rusty some nice, warm paragraphs which were genuine and true.

Eisenhower had a way of always making long lists of people he considered great. He enjoyed doing this for whatever reason. It always started with General Marshall at the top and obviously, George Washington was very high at the top also. Among people he'd known, Marshall outranked everyone. Winston Churchill was up there in the stratosphere. Toward the end of one of his volumes, he had a long list of the great people he'd known. I looked down the list. He had put Franklin Roosevelt in there. I said, "Mr. President, there's one name conspicuously missing in this list, and that's the name of Harry Truman." And he bridled because he had some misgivings about Harry Truman and he had expressed them very openly. I said that's fine, you can leave Truman's name out and put Lewis Strauss' name in, or Ernest Bevin's name in and leave Truman out. That's okay if that's what you want, but just take a look at it. And he thought for a minute. Then he said, "Oh, hell, go ahead and put Truman's name in there." And so Truman ended up on the list and I think that's probably proper. Incidentally, I like to remember the association between Eisenhower and Truman as I believe it ended in fact; and that is with their meeting at Blair House at the time of the Kennedy funeral. The two ex-presidents were invited down to go to the funeral and they went to lunch at Blair House. John was there and Margaret was there and Eisenhower and Truman. Eisenhower said to Truman, "You know, I think the differences between us have been much exaggerated and I'd like to let bygones be bygones;" and they had one lovely luncheon, full of good spirit and good memories, and the people who were there remember that. I think it was bad to start to publish the stuff which I believe must have been written by Harry Truman before that luncheon and put into some deep freeze. Now all of a sudden, in the year 1988 or 1989 or whatever it is, out comes Truman on why he didn't like Ike. I like to think of them in reconciliation because when you look at the postwar years of 1945 to 1961, what those two men did together and individually is really quite a remarkable thing. I think it shows a great consonance of conviction and loyalty and devotion to country. I think it's a beautiful thing.

The best example I suppose I can give of Eisenhower's really feeling one way and ending up writing differently is on the unlikely subject of Alaskan statehood. For some reason, Eisenhower had gone up to Alaska in 1946, and he had nearly frozen to death. He had an awful time. He went up there, the ground was frozen, the oil was frozen (you had to warm it up to get it out of the ground), and he thought, "This is for the birds. Alaska Statehood? Why make a state out of this terrible place?" That was his view, his visceral view coming into the presidency and, believe me, he maintained that view throughout his first term. There was one Assistant Secretary of the Interior and others who went in to see him one day. Ike did what he usually did; he looked up and said, "Well, what are you fellows in here for?" It was a way to scare them, put them on their mettle and make them really hold onto something if they believed in it. He felt if they didn't hold on to their belief, he had no interest in it. This Assistant Secretary kind of blanched and said, "Well, we're here to talk about statehood for Alaska, Mr. President." Ike looked at him and he said, "Well, it better be God damn good;" and he shot it down. He did not agree with the premise that we should have that statehood. Unfortunately for him, in his second term, he appointed as Secretary of the Interior, Fred Seaton. Fred had served in the United States Senate and had made his maiden speech on-guess what subject?—statehood for Alaska. Fred was committed to statehood for Alaska. He believed in it. He believed, contrary to what many Republicans thought that, if Alaska came in as a state, it would be a Republican state and indeed it has *been* a Republican state. And so Fred was out to make Alaska a state and believe me, was up against heavy odds, uphill all the way against the visceral interests of the President. He and Senator Ted Stevens of Alaska, his right hand man throughout all this, who is really THE surviving Eisenhower appointee today still in high position in the United States Congress, Ted was Fred's assistant and later became Solicitor in the Department of the Interior, those two men, almost singlehandedly, brought Alaska into the Union. Well, that was fine with Eisenhower because bringing Alaska in meant you could bring in Hawaii and that gave him quite a number of brownie points. I mean, that's a big thing for a President to do! But when we get to writing it up in the memoirs, all his old visceral feelings came back. He talked about why Alaska shouldn't have been a state. And so, what did we do? We sent the chapter to Fred Seaton for review and asked Fred what he thought of it. Well, Fred nearly had a heart attack. He was sitting out there in Nebraska thinking, this is one of the great Eisenhower victories. So he flies to Gettysburg to see the President. Fred had called me and told me, "You can't go with this kind of description of statehood for Alaska;" so I had started working on it. By the time he saw President Eisenhower, Eisenhower said, "Fred, don't worry about that, I think Bill's doing it all over again." And, indeed, we did revise it. So Alaska becomes a cardinal accomplishment for the Eisenhower Administration, as indeed it deserved to be. Fred Seaton would never have made it by himself and Ted Stevens wouldn't have made it by himself, the two of them worked in Eisenhower's name; they were working for the boss; and what happens in his Presidency reflects glory on the man at the top. Just as the goofs that happen reflect on the man at the top. So, we must give Eisenhower full credit for bringing into statehood a state that he didn't think, in his heart of hearts, really deserved to be a state.

When you talk about modifying views a bit, I found the thing most compelling in working for Eisenhower was his fidelity to fact; his absolute interest in assuring that what he set down was factually accurate and factually defensible and fair. Now, I'll give you one example and it's a compelling example.

When we got to the description of the Open Skies Proposal of 1955, the President said, "I'll do the draft of that chapter." And he went away and he did a draft which, when it came back said, "When I went to Geneva in 1955, I had this idea of Open Skies. I thought it would be a great thing if we had overflights over the Soviet Union and they had overflights over the United States. I sprang this idea on Bulganin and Khrushchev and it was an idea that electrified the whole world. I was very pleased that I had thought this up." He went on like that. Some of us had misgivings about that, having heard that it had really happened a little bit differently. What we did was to send the draft out again for review; this was our safety net. We sent it to a gentleman named Nelson Rockefeller. Now, Nelson Rockefeller had really thought up the idea of Open Skies. He had gone down to Quantico, Virginia, with a brain trust crowd, and they sat around and devised this plan. He had come back and Foster Dulles had shot it down. It wasn't going anywhere. At the last minute, Eisenhower and Dulles called for it in Geneva and sprang it on the Russians. Nelson was really the man who deserved the credit as the originator. So, what do you do? You've got Eisenhower's own draft and you have Nelson's misgivings. We didn't hear from Nelson Rockefeller for a long time. Finally, we got in touch with him and he wrote back and he said, "I hadn't written back because I didn't know what to respond. My own recollection is very different from the President's and I'm enclosing some documents written at the time of the Geneva Conference which, I think, substantiate my view." He sent along this thick file of memoranda which indeed showed him as the architect of the proposal. So we sat down and wondered how you "bell the cat" on this one. We took those drafts and simply rewrote the Eisenhower draft to conform to the Nelson Rockefeller memoranda and then we took them to the President. We said, "Mr. President, you wrote it this way and Nelson understands it differently and here are the documents written at the time that seem to bear out Nelson's recollection. You tell us which way to go." And he said, "Well, your memory plays tricks on you and I agree if those are the documents, those are the facts, why that's the way it's got to be." And that's the way it was.

Now that was a key proposal, one that was really monumental and electrifying and he began to think that he had thought of it himself and was very proud of it. All of a sudden, here a couple of flunkies who work for him come along and tell him, "Mr. President, you've got it all wrong," and he didn't bat an eye. His original draft went in the wastebasket and we used the later draft on that central issue.

When we did the two volumes, we were very proud of them for all the reasons I've enumerated. Were the historians convinced? You bet your life they were not. Absolutely not. John has said people will come up to him and ask him about X, Y, or Z event in the Eisenhower Presidency and John will say, "Well we covered all of that in the memoirs." The books, to John's view, have simply not been read. Beyond that, the historians and the critics and the media and the various people who are watching and evaluating presidents, simply did not believe Dwight Eisenhower when he said something.

I'll give you a perfect example of how his saying something can kill it. In recent revisionism, there is a quotation that appears again and again about Eisenhower. It is supposed to prove, and I think it does prove, how shrewd he was and how cautious and careful and sharp he was in handling his press conferences. There was a particular question that was going to come up in a press conference and most of his staff people urged him to duck it. Jim Hagerty said, "You'd better just duck that question, Mr. President." Eisenhower turned to him and said, "Jim, don't worry. If that question comes up, I'll just confuse them." Now you'll see that quoted again and again and again. That quotation appeared in Eisenhower's own volume one of the memoirs and John and I got it one afternoon when we sent a chapter down to Andy Goodpaster to review. Andy came up; he was going through the memoirs and making changes and he said, "There's one story you ought to put in here." He said, "It's the story about how Eisenhower said during the Quemoy and Matsu crisis, 'If that question comes up, I'll just confuse them.'" We thought, great we'll put it in and we did. Did anybody give Eisenhower credit for being shrewd and canny and so on? Not on your life. But later on, when it gets quoted by other people, later historians, it becomes evident that he's a smart gentleman. Well, look back in the memoirs.

They didn't believe Eisenhower. They didn't believe Eisenhower when he was quoting national security records, when he was quoting his own letters to Swede Hazlett; when he was quoting his own memoranda for the record; when he was quoting his own diary entries to himself; when he was quoting letters to personal friends. They didn't believe him. They also didn't believe other early Eisenhower books, and some of them were rather "stuffed shirtish," I will say. Ezra Benson's book? There were a lot of punches pulled; Lewis Strauss', the same thing. Sherman Adams' book, *Firsthand Report*, was pretty controlled and pretty sanitized; not really telling all. They believed Emmet Hughes because Emmet condemned Eisenhower's foreign policy but they did not believe the part of Emmet Hughes' book that I think is to this day really valuable and that is the insights into Eisenhower, the man. It's wonderful. There are direct quotes which Emmet Hughes thinks proved one thing and I think really showed Eisenhower off very, very nobly and brilliantly. They didn't believe Arthur Larson in 1968, who wrote *Eisenhower: the President Nobody Knew*. Arthur had a very, very straight view of Eisenhower, and still critics were not convinced. There was no revisionism. For revisionism, I think you need two things: you need, in the first place, the access of independent scholars, who, unlike the rest of us, don't have that personal association but have access to the sources that President Eisenhower himself used. That is the process that has been going on in recent years. The more scholars get into the documents, the more they read the letters to Hazlett, the more they look at the NSC papers, the more they look at that personal correspondence, the more they realize he's telling the truth; that's the way it was. A light goes on. It's like a special prosecutor or a counselor going in there independently. Some of these people began as Stevenson Democrats and they came out on the other side. But you need something else despite the fact that all of us, as historians, love to think that we changed everything and revised everything. I don't think historians really do it that much.

What really has made Eisenhower revisionism is the second thing that has to have happened: a passage of time. Eisenhower always believed you judge a President not by what he did at the moment but by what happens after him. He always said if the South had won the Civil War, what would our opinion be today of President "X"? Everyone thinks Lincoln...he wasn't talking about Lincoln, he was talking about George Washington. George Washington would have been the Father of a little country up here in the North with another country down in the South, or something of the sort. He would have modified his place in history. So you should judge Eisenhower by what has happened since and I don't need to belabor this.

Take it decade by decade. In the 1960's, you judge Eisenhower against Vietnam. And a light begins to go on. If you go back into 1954, you find that he stayed out of Vietnam. We sank up to our eyebrows in Vietnam in the 1960's. In the 1970's, we had double digit inflation. Eisenhower thought that if inflation got up to about 2%, the country was going down the tube. He had an inflation rate over eight years of about 1.4% In the 1980's, what did we have? A $200 billion budget deficit. What do you compare those against? You compare those against Eisenhower's three balanced budgets out of the four that we've had in nearly 40 years; and the fourth one is an accident. You give Eisenhower credit for keeping his eye on a balanced budget. We are in inordinate trouble today because of those deficits. Now, you can't go through Vietnam, double digit inflation, $200 billion deficits and not look back at a man who had no Vietnam, had three balanced budgets and 1.4% inflation and not think well, just possibly, some revisionism is in order. I think basically that has been the major thing that you measure him against.

Look into the 1990's. What have we got? We don't know what we're going to have. It could be a Golden Era. It could be something different. You know, you have an event at the present time, in the Persian Gulf. How can you measure Eisenhower against it? You measure Eisenhower against it by the way he conducted United States policy in Lebanon in 1958, where he went in with the most massive buildup of American forces, emergency forces, in the history of the country to date. He called for UN action and he pledged that, once the UN acted, he'd get out. That's what you measure the current Gulf crisis against. The jury's out and the story remains open and it may turn out to be an enormous success story. There is no telling what else will come up that you'll measure him against. Some things could be negative, but I think that's the measurement and I think that, more than anything else, accounts for the revisionism that our little group here tried to launch back in January or February of 1961.

Now, I see I've spoken a bit long. I'll be glad to answer questions and I assume that with an audience like this, there are a lot of questions, so let me just stop at that point. If no one asks a question, I'll keep on talking.

I realize I'm the only thing between you and the happy hour.

R. J. Watson: I'm R. J. Watson, in the office of the Secretary of Defense and happen to be writing a history of the Department of Defense in the second Eisenhower administration and I've been very interested in the remark you quote in your book in which Eisenhower said he wondered how Charlie Wilson ever became President of a large corporation and it's never been clear to me why Ike seemed to be so much harder on his secretary, Wilson, than he was on McElroy. Can you explain that? He once publicly praised McElroy but I don't think he ever praised Wilson.

Dr. William Ewald: This is like many statements that Eisenhower made and I think you have to allow him to make them. As Herbert Brownell said, he would sound off in cocktail party conversation and sometimes he would get mad at people for whom he had an enormous respect. I think he had a great respect for Charlie Wilson; otherwise, Charlie Wilson would not have remained Secretary of Defense from '53 to '57. As an historian, these statements intrigue me. I did have that statement reported to me by a man who obviously had Eisenhower's confidence and to whom Eisenhower had said it. I think Charlie Wilson had a way, as Eisenhower said, of taking people on a short trip around the world. He could talk at great length and it was very hard to stop him. Sometimes these things annoyed, nettled Eisenhower. Let me give you another quote to balance that out because I don't think it's fair to the memory of Charlie Wilson. He *did* admire Neil McElroy greatly. Also, Eisenhower always said that, in each crisis, when you've got a face to face confrontation with the Russians, "I never thought that when push came to shove, when the showdown came, that the Russians would ever do a damned thing and neither did Charlie Wilson." I think that shows his respect for Charlie Wilson's judgment. I would not use that any more than I would use an offhand remark about Earl Warren or William Brennan as the end opinion of Dwight Eisenhower. I think you have to take them all, and historians, when somebody tells them something like that, snap it up. I plead guilty because it is a lively comment and it did happen but it's not the whole story.

Robert Shogan: My name is Robert Shogan. I'm a reporter for the *Los Angeles Times*, Washington Bureau. I read, like many other people, your op-ed piece in the *New York Times*, drawing on the Eisenhower experiences, sort of in terms of what he might have done or perhaps what President Bush should have done in the Persian Gulf. I wonder if you could use that same approach and perhaps find some lesson or suggestions for President Bush in terms of his current domestic "pickle" in dealing with the Congress and unsnarling this budget package and putting it back together again. How would Eisenhower have handled this kind of business?

Dr. William Ewald: You know, I don't know. I think it's such a mess, such a colossal mess and that there's so much blame to be spread around—the Executive Branch and the Legislative Branch. Let me say, Eisenhower did have a divided government. He had an opposition party in control of the Senate and the House after January, 1955 to 1961, and he really felt that he had to work with these people. I wouldn't say this as a final judgment, but he didn't particularly like Lyndon Johnson or particularly like Sam Rayburn the way he liked some other people. On the other hand, they controlled the Senate, they controlled the House and, if he was going to get anything done *particularly* in national security affairs, but also on budgetary affairs and domestic policy, he had to work with them.

And so he was very, very solicitous of them. He told Lyndon Johnson and Sam Rayburn to come down to the White House. They could come down whenever they wanted. They would go upstairs in the mansion and they would have a drink with the President at five o'clock in the afternoon and they would kick things around privately, just the three of them. He had his very, very trusted Secretary of the Treasury, Robert Anderson, who was a Texan, as an emissary to both Johnson and Rayburn. He leaned over backwards to work carefully with them without abandoning principle; for example, they had some very, very keen differences of opinion, especially on the budget and on spending in those last two years. Eisenhower fought the Democrats to a standstill on that; but basically, he never lost touch with them. I think the process to unsnarl what happened starts a long way back. You try to establish some kind of working relationship and hope you would never get yourself into this kind of colossal problem that is just tearing the country to pieces. That may not be the right kind of answer but he was most conciliatory and most cooperative.

William Moore: I'm William Moore from the University of Wyoming and I have a question concerning Eisenhower and historians. One of the sources that historians have used recently to try to get at the "inner Eisenhower" are the Swede Hazlett letters. There's a quality about those letters that I think struck some historians as almost contrived. Obviously they are letters from Eisenhower to Hazlett but there's a sense in which Eisenhower seems to almost be speaking to historians. He's writing the letters to Hazlett almost as if he's leaving some kind of written message or written self-justification for historians. I know that this is not just my idea, there are a number of conversations I've had with several historians here and I wondered it you would simply talk about the Hazlett letters as a historical source.

Dr. William Ewald: You mean that he was consciously leaving a trail?

William Moore: Yes.

Dr. William Ewald: I don't think that he was doing it in the way you say. Teddy Roosevelt wrote letters to his children realizing that future historians were going to snap them up and make something of them. The reason I don't believe that Ike's was a conscious, deliberate effort is that he was so haphazard about it. You know, months would go by between letters and then he'd get a letter and all of a sudden he'd write two or three and then stop. He could have done it maybe with his diary entries, but it was a hit and miss thing. Sometimes he'd say something, sometimes he wouldn't. When we'd ask him what was it about Swede Hazlett that elicited this kind of letter from him, he'd say Swede was the kind of guy whom, when you were ready to blow your stack, you could really sound off against. Most of these things were Eisenhower "pounding the table" and getting mad, blowing his stack against somebody or expressing extreme exasperation with individuals and short-sighted people in the government. That seems to be the characteristic thing rather than his attempt to say, "Now I'm doing this and I'm doing that for this reason;" hoping historians would pick it up.

I will tell you that, as a historian, I wish Eisenhower had left a lot more records and a lot more of a trail than he did. But, personally, he left a very magnificent trail with General Goodpaster and the notes that Goodpaster kept and the notes of the NSC meetings kept by the staff people over there. Those were magnificent. Eisenhower, himself, really was an honest man. He would blow up one day and the next day, not. So I don't see any ulterior motive in that but I'm surely glad that he did those things.

Brad Patterson: Bill, I'm your old colleague in the White House Staff, Brad Patterson.

Dr. William Ewald: I was going to say, Brad, you're out of bounds. You're not allowed to ask questions. You know too much.

Brad Patterson: I wanted to ask a different question. I wanted to ask you about your perception of the ethics problem in writing books about the presidency. We've both written some, you more than I. What do you think as a historian, knowing the value, just as you were saying, of paper trails, what do you think is the line as a time point before which it's unethical or inappropriate to write quick "kiss and tell" books about the presidency, about presidents I have counselled, or the country I have helped run and at which point in the hump of history is it appropriate to do so? Now you, of course, had the experience of working here with Number One, the ex-President himself. We've had experience recently of books that have come out from the Reagan White House by people even before their President left office. A gentleman like Andy Goodpaster probably will not write a book nor will Bill Hopkins. Others have written books, of course, with much immediacy, with much personal insight, personal experience, which are invaluable as history. Everybody on the White House staff, by giving an oral history, writes something and at some point, those oral histories become written in the public domain. So, to repeat, what do you think as to the ethics, the propriety, the valued history weighing these two things of the memoirs of those people who do that? To put the question in a tougher way, if you were President, what instructions would you give your staff about writing books?

Dr. William Ewald: Well, understand, I would not do it, but I understand that Lyndon Johnson did. He was on his Air Force One airplane and he saw people scribbling down notes. He'd go up and down the aisle and take all the notes out of their hand and stuff them in his pocket and say, "These belong to me."

I would like to quote scripture. I will not quote it directly because I've forgotten the quotation but there's nothing said which shall remain hidden, there is nothing done which will not be shouted from the housetops. That was either the Sermon on the Mount or something close to it. In the end, I believe for the good of the country, and the good of the world, that every fact, and underscore *every fact that it's possible to know*, should become known in the end. The question is: where's the end? I mean, I do not see hiding anything. I think, for people who are dead, they can only hurt the people who are living who come after them who might profit by their example. Okay, that's number one.

But short of that, the question is where and when do you break that? I think that the President had a perfect right not to bare his soul and spill everything that he wanted to spill about everybody if that's what he chose. I think that I will mention my own experience. We worked through these memoirs and when we'd finished, I felt that there were a lot of things said in the memoirs that he did not want to say about himself, for one reason or another, that I *could* say; and so, I did a short piece and I called it "Ike and Myths and History" very much more aggressively, in a sense, defending his record. I showed that to him and he was delighted. He said he wouldn't do it but he was delighted to have me do it. I'm sure he would have been delighted to have somebody else do it and he would be delighted with the revisionist history that's going on and so he felt that, sure, you go and you tell the truth. I wouldn't have done it if, for example, I felt that what I was going to do was turn around and say, "Well now, here's this man who has presented a false image to the country and let me tell you what he was really like. He was really a stinker," and you run him down. I think that's disloyal. I think that any person who feels that way during the time he works for the president, and I would definitely and specifically include the man I just praised a few minutes ago, Emmet Hughes, should resign and should not continue in the president's confidence. I think that's an abuse of that confidence and I think that's the place where he should get out. He can then be on the outside and say whatever he likes from his vantage point but not use inside information.

I will say that, when I did my first book, *Eisenhower the President*, I didn't show it to the family. I didn't show it to John. I didn't show it to Milton. I didn't show it to anybody. I published it and then sent them copies. Milton was very, very glowing in his praise for the book. He said I had done an enormous amount of good, more good at that time than any other. That was early. John said the same things: You don't spare the warts but you hit the big things. They felt, in a sense, that it was a loyal book, that it went beyond what Eisenhower himself might have said, and that it was revealing in a way that I hoped could possibly help future citizens of the country to judge the President.

Now, I will give you an example of bad timing. I mentioned Margaret Truman. Margaret Truman is coming out and publishing her father's anti-Ike diatribe. If, at the beginning, Margaret Truman had said, "My father wrote this way back and he was feeling bad, having been displaced, put out of the White House by Eisenhower, and he was angry with Eisenhower and he was sounding off against him, and here's what he wrote at the time," dated it and said, here's Harry Truman, such and such a date; if Margaret had said, "X years after that, I went to a luncheon with President Eisenhower, my father and John. We had a great time and there was a reconciliation," then at least you've got an honest story and sooner or later I suppose historians will catch up with the chronology of that. I don't see suppressing the Truman diatribe; for that reason, I say publish it, put a date on it, and show how he modified his views over time. I guess I'd get back to the original point that, as a historian, I think you publish anything that is factual. As a member of a president's staff, as an associate with him, you do not abuse that privilege for the purposes of publishing your own book and making money. You know perfectly well, there are people who get on campaign planes and campaign with the candidate and when the candidate wins, the writer splits off, says so long, I'm off to the publishers to tell what you're really like—the new President going in. That has happened and it's bad practice and I don't like that kind of abuse. I don't know if that's an answer but I think it's where you have to come out.

Bill Railing: I'm Bill Railing. I'm on the faculty at the college here. Would you mind elaborating a bit on Eisenhower's views on inflation? You referred to it at the end that if inflation got to 2%, Eisenhower thought the country was finished. Would you be able to elaborate on that a bit?

Dr. William Ewald: You have to remember that when Eisenhower came into office, and if you look back to 1945, 1952, the value of the dollar, the consumer price index (I always get this wrong; Richard Nixon used to get it wrong in his speeches too), the consumer price index went up 50%, the value of a dollar went down. Nixon used to say it was cut in half. It wasn't cut in half, it was cut by a third. We had a legacy of bad inflation in the immediate postwar years and this really scared Eisenhower and it scared all of his administration. They were determined to fight inflation by holding down federal spending and that's the principal way they held it down. They also had a Fed chairman, an independent Democrat, a friendly Democrat, our kind of Democrat, William McChesney Martin, who really helped to hold prices down. And between the two of them, they worked and they accomplished this result. But they felt that inflation, as Arthur Burns says, at 3% a year over 30 years is going to wipe out a whole generation and it's terrible. Well, now, if it gets down to 3%, we think we're in great shape. So, he felt very, very strongly about this and, frankly, in the last years of his presidency, after the 1958 Congressional elections which produced a lopsided Democratic majority in Congress, he really dug in his heels and was determined to submit a balanced budget and fight them every step of the way. Indeed he did, with his little cadre of Republicans and a number of southern Democrats and it was a real point of great importance for him and, frankly, most people didn't care. Against catching up with the Russians, the Russians are coming, missile gaps, Sputnik, get America moving again, what did a balanced budget matter? You don't know until now. As Winston Churchill said, people ask, what are we fighting for in World War II, and he said, "If we stop, you'll find out." And we have found out.

If I may tell you one last story, because it's about working for Eisenhower and people say, wasn't it great to work for a man who had a nice grin and who would slap you on the back? Eisenhower didn't grin at us very much, it was hard work all the time, he was all business and he didn't slap you on the back. He had a way of arriving at the office at 8:00 o'clock in the morning, and he would start in on the manuscript. If he was there by himself, he'd start in on it. If he had one person with him, he'd start in on it.

Sam Vaughn and I tended to work late at night after the President would go home about 5:30 or 6:00; we'd work late. One night, we worked until midnight or thereafter and we dragged in at about 8:03 the next morning. Eisenhower was sitting there with his manuscript, ready to go and writing in his emendations. He looked up at us and said, "You fellas may work late, but you get up late too." And I think that's the greatest compliment I ever had. Thank you very much.

CHAPTER SIX

Eisenhower as Leader

Six scholars on the Eisenhower Presidency were brought together in this panel to assess the leadership skills of President Eisenhower. Among the panelists were President Eisenhower's biographer, Stephen Ambrose, and his grandson, David Eisenhower.

David Eisenhower argues that the primary agenda of the Eisenhower administration was foreign policy. He was elected to defuse the cold war and, as a result, spent two thirds of his time on issues of national security, test bans and disarmament, and curbing the Soviet Union. David Eisenhower believes that his grandfather's greatest leadership skills were in the international arena.

Dr. R. Gordon Hoxie, a close associate of President Eisenhower and currently President of the Center for the Study of the Presidency, believes that the Eisenhower legacy is broader than the international arena. He cites, for example, President Eisenhower's skills with Congress in pushing through legislation creating NASA and the Defense Reorganization Bill. Dr. Hoxie argues that President Eisenhower was a master politician who skillfully pressured Congress to support his legislation. Fred Greenstein, author of one of the most important works on the Eisenhower presidency, entitled *The Hidden Hand Presidency,* supports the Hoxie view. According to Dr. Greenstein, President Eisenhower did not want to be characterized as a "politician." His image as a statesman and leader catapulted him to an average 64% approval rating throughout his presidency, the highest of any president. Yet Dr. Greenstein notes that President Eisenhower was a skillful politician, who was able to maneuver situations in his favor often through intermediaries.

The clear consensus of the scholars in this forum was that

President Eisenhower was a master statesman, and as such was a master politician. His strength was in his ability to balance one idea against another, of not being an extremist, and of ensuring that long range objectives were not obscured by short range rewards.

PANEL

Moderator: **Louis Galambos,** *Professor of History and Editor, "The Papers of Dwight D. Eisenhower," Johns Hopkins University*

Panelists:

Fred I. Greenstein   *Professor, Woodrow Wilson School of Public International Affairs, Princeton University*

D. David Eisenhower   *Historian and Author*

R. Gordon Hoxie   *President, Center for the Study of the Presidency*

Phillip G. Henderson   *Professor, University of Maryland, Baltimore County*

Stephen Ambrose   *Director, University of New Orleans Eisenhower Center for Leadership Studies*

Louis Galambos: Thank you very much. This *is* a distinguished panel and I'm honored to be a moderator for this group of people. They have all agreed, some reluctantly, to throw away the lengthy papers they wrote so that they won't read anything to you. What they have all agreed to do is to talk a little, very briefly, about what they see as the strongest aspect of President Eisenhower's leadership and then the aspect of which they are the most critical. Our first speaker is first among equals of the biographers of Dwight David Eisenhower, my former handball opponent. He always beat me. Stephen Ambrose is an outstanding historian and biographer of Ike and of Richard Nixon.

Stephen Ambrose: Thank you, Lou. We just got this assignment literally seconds ago, folks, and I had this beautiful speech here ready to give to you and he's not going to let me do it. But I will talk about what I think is the strongest aspect of Ike's leadership. I think that was his character. Now, what was the source of his character? He was the last President born in the

19th century and it seems to me that that's a key in understanding Dwight Eisenhower. Those late Victorians were quite
remarkable men. They fought the first World War, they got the
country through the Depression without sacrificing democracy,
they led us through the Second World War, created the doctrine
of containment, and provided the defense establishment and
made it work. Thanks to that generation, Naziism and Communism are now on the ash heap of history, unmourned.

In Ike's case, his Victorian background was reinforced by
West Point and military education. I pause here to make this
point. You know, Charles de Gaulle is five weeks younger than
Dwight Eisenhower and will be celebrating his 100th birthday
next month. That leads to this observation: Isn't it remarkable
that three of the greatest leaders of the greatest democracies of
the 20th century, Ike, de Gaulle and Winston Churchill, all had
military educations? In any case, these Victorians had charac-
ters that were as solid as a rock. They were men who spurned
all temptations and they kept their noses to the grindstone.
They were men of awesome will power. One thinks of Ike, who
once smoked four packs of cigarettes a day, quitting "cold turkey" in 1948 and never touching tobacco again. In the library in
Abilene, there's a wonderful agenda for the 1960 Paris summit,
the one that Khrushchev broke up, on the back of which Ike
wrote, when Khrushchev was engaging in a tirade, "God, I wish
I had a cigarette." But he was strong enough to resist it. These
Victorians, and *very much* so with Ike, were trustworthy. Their
word was their bond. Monty said it best about Ike. He said, "Ike
has but to smile at you and you trust him at once. He has the
power of attracting the hearts of men as the magnet attracts the
bits of metal."

I spent more than twenty years studying Ike, reading his
letters, his memos, his memoirs, his cables and so forth; and I've
only caught him in two lies. One was in 1944, when he lied to
Adolph Hitler about where he was going to invade. The second
was in 1960, when he lied to Nikita Khrushchev about what
Francis Gary Powers was doing in his air space. Ike, like most
of those Victorian men, would no more cheat on his income tax
than he would defect to the Soviet Union. He was a man who
had the deepest respect for others so long as they met their

responsibilities and did their duty. His own sense of duty was very strong even before he went to West Point; it was obviously reinforced by West Point and his army career. He had, and this seems to me also to be typical of that generation of men, a very strong sense of the rightness and wrongness of things; a sense of propriety, if you wish.

In 1945, Hollywood offered him a big, fat contract if they could make a biography of him and make a movie out of it. Mamie was all for it. She was tired of pinching pennies as she had been doing for the last thirty-five years. Ike just flat turned it down. He said he could have no respect for anyone who made money out of a position of public trust. "Besides," he told Mamie, "it's fun to be poor.

Now, to go to the negative side. These Victorians had their faults. One of them was sexism. It was characteristic of the Victorian men to take women for granted and to have a sense that there is a *place* for women and that is clearly defined and is the *only* place for them. This was true of Ike, I regret to say. He was a male chauvinist. The best example, known to all the scholars in this room, is Ann Whitman, the greatest secretary imaginable. She gave up her marriage and any life of her own for eight years for Ike, and he never even noticed her. He just took for granted that she should slave for him.

Another weakness of those Victorians was a rampant racism. Now, I'm not going to accuse Ike of being a rampant racist, but he certainly was a segregationist. He was born, one needs to remind oneself, six (6) years before the Supreme Court declared in *Plessy v. Ferguson* that separate but equal was the law of the land. Ike agreed with *Plessy v. Ferguson* far more than he ever agreed with *Brown v. Topeka*. He never spoke up for *Brown v. Topeka* and I think that was one of his biggest shortcomings as a leader. There, I did it in five minutes.

Louis Galambos: Thank you, Steve, you never disappoint me. Our next speaker is a distinguished, young political scientist, a student of the Presidency and author of *Managing the Presidency*, Phillip Henderson.

Phillip Henderson: Thank you. I think Eisenhower's greatest strength, at least as President, and I suppose this carries over into his role as a General, was his knack for organization and his belief as President that the office of the Presidency is bigger than any one person. This belief transcended the Rooseveltian view that one person could be in charge of everything. I think that John F. Kennedy and Lyndon Johnson tended to try to go back to the Rooseveltian notion that the President alone can be in charge of the institution of the Presidency and can make major decisions with a small group of advisors. Eisenhower incorporated a regular, organized process in the White House. Eisenhower's administrative innovations throughout his Presidency, including the creation of staff and Cabinet secretariats, the use of the first formally dedicated White House Chief of Staff, the creation of the Special Assistant for National Security Affairs position, and many other innovations, tended to reinforce the view that he believed you needed the broad input of the departments, the assistance of the experts in the bureaucracy and the knowledge that comes from the institutional memory and expertise of the vast federal government. I think Eisenhower utilized the departments better than any other President before or since.

I think that perhaps his greatest weakness, which Richard Neustadt alluded to in his book, *Presidential Power,* was that Eisenhower did not care as much as he should have about Washington reputation. He allowed people to believe that he was not in charge of his administration when, in fact, as we now know, thanks to Fred Greenstein, Stephen Ambrose, and others, that he *was* in charge at every level. He always knew the broad outlines of policies, and many times much to the amazement of even his own staff, many of the details of important policies. I think his inability to communicate his successes as President, by not establishing a formal office of White House communications in the modern day sense, an office that could do damage control every time a negative story came out about his administration and promote his administration in a way that would have enhanced his reputation among those in Congress and in the Washington and the journalistic communities, hindered his Presidency. I think that was a weakness of Eisenhower's. He simply was not a person who was interested in taking credit for those things he accomplished.

Louis Galambos: Thank you, it's very interesting that our next contributor is unique to this panel. He's the only person on our panel who has, himself, been a president. He was the President of C. W. Post College and Chancellor of Long Island University and is a prolific editor and author on the Presidency in the United States—R. Gordon Hoxie.

R. Gordon Hoxie: Thank you, Lou. It is wonderful to be on board here, and I just might say, since you make to generous reference to my work in studying the Presidency, that the inspiration for it came from our subject, President Eisenhower. I had a modest role as an educational aide when he was at Columbia University, and we kept in touch through the years. In early 1968, he wrote a very interesting memorandum on the importance of studying the Presidency, and that gave me the inspiration for establishing the Center for the Study of the Presidency.

Let me just say this. I believe that President Eisenhower's great strength was in his ability to command and his ability to get the best from all of those who worked with him. There was never a doubt as to who was in command. It is true that he worked effectively with the Congress. I think that was his strength. Political scientists have only recently discovered that which his public has always known, that the most effective relationships, the best bipartisanships we have ever had in the modern Presidency, were in the Eisenhower years. It has, regrettably, been downhill ever since. When the gauntlet was laid down by the Congress, he could be strong. Let me give you an example. He asked several people to look at reorganization of the Defense Department, such as Nelson Rockefeller and others. Finally in 1958, he made up his mind that it had to be done and he sat down and rewrote a reorganization program himself. He took the service secretaries out of the chain of command, and you can imagine what that meant. They went to all of their groups, whether it was the Air Force Association, the Army, or the Navy and they went charging up the Hill to Congress. Congress, which had always been very gentle and kind and respectful, was referring to him as trying to use Prussian tactics to force something through. Well, with the gauntlet laid down, he said to his Press Secretary, Jim Hagerty, whom, everyone will agree, is the best Press Secretary we've ever had, "I want you to get together editors, large and small, and I want to talk heart-to-heart with them." He got a thousand editors together; the editorials that poured forth were just marvelous in support of his reorganization plan. Then he said to his friends, "I want you to write letters." The Congress had never been so blitzed; thousands and thousands of letters descended on the Congress. The Congress caved in. The Reorganization Act of 1958 was personally written and personally won by Dwight Eisenhower.

One other example in the same year was NASA. The armed forces and many people were much opposed to NASA. Johnson, who was no slouch himself, said, "How are you going to get this thing through?" He got it through the Pentagon so fast that these were Johnson's words, "Ike must have carried it through the Pentagon on a motorcycle."

These are some examples of his strengths. The third example I want to present is his moral and spiritual leadership. More than any other President except Lincoln, he looked at leadership in moral and spiritual terms, just like the "Emancipator," whose name will long endure in Gettysburg. As he expressed it, "America is not good because it is great, America is great because it is good." He believed that so fervently. In the event there is a weakness in Eisenhower, and it's hard for me to find it, it was his overwhelmingly sincere belief in good in almost everyone. He was not naive; rather he was a good judge of men. But, and I can attest to this, he could perhaps even be too kind.

Louis Galambos: Our next speaker is a former sports writer-become-historian and a biographer of his grandfather—David Eisenhower.

David Eisenhower: Thank you, Lou. Our topic is Eisenhower as a Leader, pluses and minuses. I am a family member so I'm going to set myself up as somewhat of an exception about this. I have trouble finding minuses and I see lots of pluses. Let me suggest an approach on the subject. Eisenhower as leader. What is leadership? Leadership is explained by the famous saying, "I can't define it, but I know it when I see it." My question is: Where do you look for strengths? Where do you look for weaknesses in Dwight Eisenhower as a leader? I would argue that the Presidency, as an institution, is a mission-oriented job. It is a mission-oriented job in that, in order to understand a given President, the process begins by trying to frame the overriding issue that accounts for the election of that President and accounts for the dynamics of his administration. Why was Dwight D. Eisenhower leader of the United States? He was elected in 1952 for many personal reasons, many of which have been put forth by the panel already today. He was honest, he was straightforward, he was popular, he was a hero; but above all, the overriding issue facing American people in 1952 was the Cold War and the overriding need in those circumstances was for a figure of the Alliance, someone who understood how the United States, Great Britain and the Soviet Union had, only seven years before, managed to co-exist and even to cooperate, in the joint venture against Germany. This was the mission of his Presidency as I see it. It was also his mission in the Korean War, as it was to launch initiatives in the 1950's aimed at defusing the Cold War. This was what he was equipped to do. As a result, if one were to look for pluses in the Eisenhower record as a leader, I would look in that area. This is precisely why he was placed in the Presidency. I would say that his legacy, or the Eisenhower story, really is the story of World War II: carrying out World War II, the war itself against Germany, and then assuming responsibility for the consequences. That is, assuming the burden of reconstruction in Europe and in Asia as the war was over. Dwight D. Eisenhower played a great role in that. If I were looking for outstanding attributes of leadership, I would look for it in that area.

Correspondingly, a Presidency, because it is a mission-oriented institution, is powerful and it is effective. A President is an effective leader when he is addressing the issue that he is elected to confront. He's less powerful in other areas, less effective If I were to recommend areas to look for weaknesses, I would look in those areas that the Eisenhower Administration was not elected to confront or address. Civil Rights would be one of them. Dwight D. Eisenhower was elected to defuse the Cold War and not to solve the civil rights question. He was the President of the United States and he had a broad agenda, therefore, civil rights was a responsibility. But his primary responsibility in civil rights, as I see it, was to prepare the issue in such a way that his successor, who would be the civil rights President, would have an easier time addressing that thorny and fundamental problem which was facing America in the late '50's and early '60's.

So, looking for positives, I look for the evidence of Eisenhower's leadership ability and traits and his war record. In his record as president, I believe it feels like he devoted two-thirds of his working time to issues of national security, disarmament, technical discussions about rocketry, defense reorganization, relations with the Soviets, and so forth. This is where the strengths are.

The weaknesses perhaps lay in something as simple as Dwight Eisenhower's difficulty in being all things to all people. Some Presidents are good at this.

Fred Greenstein: And as a granddad, even higher.

Louis Galambos: Thank you very much. Our next speaker is an eminent political scientist. He has had as much to do with the scholarship which now has reappraised Eisenhower and the Presidency as any person, and is most associated with the concept of the "Hidden Hand"—Fred Greenstein of Princeton University.

Fred Greenstein: Picking up where David left off on the slipperiness of the notion of leadership, let me say that it's slippery when people say that anyone, Eisenhower or another, was a good or a bad leader; they mean two different things, and those ideas don't necessarily go together. There's leadership in a substantive sense, and there's leadership in what you might call the instrumental sense. By substantive, I mean the policies and the merits of the policies that a leader advocated and actually brought to bear. Now, there will always be disagreement about substantive leadership. Conservatives and liberals, no matter what they're called, or radicals or reactionaries, will inevitably evaluate policies that don't have any automatic solution. Should people get welfare benefits or should you throw them out to fight for their own? Is it better to be aggressive in international situations and defend your honor, or is it better to be retiring and perhaps even absorb some blows in order to survive? Those are philosophical differences, and, as a political scientist, while I have my own views, I won't presume to promulgate them to others.

Now, as far as the instrumental sense, it may seem less glorious and more Machiavellian and, therefore, contemptible, but that's the thing that we political scientists do. While other people are rhapsodic, we may look at the mechanics of the specifics.

Much of the criticism of Eisenhower in the '50's, and certainly by my generation, was on both substantive and instrumental (or mechanical) grounds. Now I think you can still find the substantive criticism, and you will continue to find it in writings about the Eisenhower Presidency. Should he have moved faster on Civil Rights? Well, Steve says "yes" and I certainly say "yes," but I see no reason why everybody else would have to say "yes."

On the instrumental side, those of us who were not as close to Eisenhower as some of the insiders—Brownell, Goodpaster and so on, whom you've seen at this meeting—really saw something which, to some extent, Eisenhower wanted us to see. We saw someone who seemed to be a popular, loved icon, but who was essentially a simple, Kansas type who had no complexity, no subtlety, and who was sufficiently detached from the tasks of leadership. We were delighted with such images as the story about the person who said, "Wouldn't it be terrible if Eisenhower died and Richard Nixon would become President?" And the other person said, "But it would be worse if Sherman Adams died and Eisenhower would become President." And we heard really cruel observations such as, "He couldn't read his briefing papers, his lips were chapped." That's the sort of thing you get about all Presidents. To some extent, people like to demean them to strengthen their own self-images if they have such needs. Now, no one, in the scholarly world who has studied what we now know as a result of declassification about Dwight Eisenhower, no matter how critical they are, thinks that he was simple-minded, inept, or unaware about political means or give-and-take. Now, I think you can no more say within his leadership style what the single strongest element is, than you can say which is the most important leg for holding up a chair. It's the fact that they complement each other. Well, one of the elements of his leadership that is underestimated in my book, and perhaps more so because at the last minute the phrase "Hidden Hand" became the label of the book, and therefore, to some extent, was the symbol of it, I think is his conceptual capacities. He was a very clear-headed man with a long-time horizon, the same mentality that made him a good military planner and probably even the same mentality that made him quite brilliant at Abilene High School in doing simple plane geometry. It's a very deductive mind, one which he often didn't even show in its elegance to people who met with him in the NSC meetings. His custom was to be much more homely in his expressions than his analytic capacities made it possible for him to be, and, if you read his correspondence, you can see what a literate man, in an unpretentious Victorian way, Dwight Eisenhower was. But he was subtle and complicated, and the "Hidden Hand" element is something which is evident. I'll give you an example of a "Hidden Hand" episode. The majority leader of the Senate is one Lyndon Baines Johnson. Lyndon Baines Johnson has met with Eisenhower and he says, "I'm going to see so and so," but he gets back to the Hill and he does so and so. We have a transcript by Ann Whitman, whom I think Ike actually did appreciate. Ann has been listening on a blind extension and she takes down the following message to Treasury Secretary Humphreys:

> *Eisenhower:* George, I want you to call Sid Richardson *(Sid Richardson is a multi-millionaire, one of these flamboyant, Texas oil types. He's the guy who put up the money that enabled Lyndon to run for office to begin with.)* Now, you tell Sid to tell Lyndon Johnson that if he doesn't straighten out in Congress, Sid Richardson will put up the money for someone named Al Shivers *(a very popular governor of Texas)* to run against him in the primaries.

Now, this totally destroys any image of somebody who doesn't think about the details of politics or doesn't have an enormously well-furnished mind in terms of political ramifications. These things are abundantly present in the twelve volumes of presidential papers that Professor Galambos has edited. There is the "Hidden Hand" element, an enormous modesty, and even a kind of reluctance to take credit—someone who is probably a virtuous Jimmy Stewart type, sort of a Kansas mode. A lot of it, I believe, comes out of his long experience of having jobs in the military that required being fundamentally the same as a political leader in the kinds of thing you had to do, but you always justify it on different grounds. Now, that's not quite lying, but it's also not quite verbally straight shooting. I believe when Eisenhower said something, he always asked "What's the best way to say that?" not, "What's the most eloquent say to say that?"

Now, I think that the down side of his Presidency was all of the underplaying of the political side. I do think it enabled him in many ways to maintain enormous adulation of the American people. No President, including Ronald Reagan, at least since FDR, and we don't have Gallup Poll figures on FDR, has been as persistently high in standing as viewed by the American people as Dwight Eisenhower was. His average Gallup support is the highest of any president, and we have those figures from Truman on, except for Kennedy, and Kennedy, of course, was truncated. Obviously, I wouldn't count Bush at the moment. His popularity has suddenly hemorrhaged rather dramatically. Now, I think this entire mode of not showing your hand has an important down side. My point will be very similar to the one which Phil Henderson made. I don't think it's so important that people didn't know that he was skilled, but I think that he under-utilized the "bully pulpit." He particularly under-utilized it in terms of giving specific analytic arguments of the sort he was capable of giving. I believe the greatest failing there is probably in the last three years of his Presidency. During the period when the Democrats were so strongly talking about the bomber gaps or the missile gaps and people were saying "we need enormous arms buildup," he said the most brilliant things about the most advanced strategic doctrine: about sufficiency in nuclear weapons and the undesirability of going beyond the minimum necessary retaliatory capacity. His messages did not get through. They did not get through effectively and that surely is part of the reason why the Kennedy Administration, including McGeorge Bundy, in retrospect, views Eisenhower as: a) having been brilliant on those matters, but b) not having promulgated them well enough. This is one reason why they went through the most extravagant escalation of military preparedness which, in many ways, is as responsible as supply side economics for the difficulties we've faced since then.

Louis Galambos: Thank you very much. David, I wanted to ask you about one of the things I think people have made more and more of in recent times. It's probably on all of our minds because of the Middle East right now, and that is Eisenhower's restraint in the exercise of power. Would you think that that was an important aspect of his Presidency?

David Eisenhower: I think it was, and I liked Fred's mention of the conceptual side of Dwight Eisenhower. I think he's somebody who had a "feel" for history. I know my father has it and I was around my granddad enough to hear it, so he had it as well. It is a feel, not only an acquaintance with, but a feel for, ancient history, for Civil War history, and so forth. He was a man of perspective and I think he had a sense for the unique situation that the United States was in in 1953 and 1954, as indeed it was in 1944 and 1945. America, during the Eisenhower years, occupied a position that no country has occupied before or since. We were the most powerful nation on earth; it was an extraordinary circumstance and I think Dwight Eisenhower conceptually understood that. What do you do with temporary advantage of that dimension? I think the way he approached it was to convert our temporary advantage into long-range benefit for the United States and, therefore, in circumstances where we enjoyed great advantages over everybody else, we would do it with restraint. That sets him apart from his predecessors as well as his successors. Ronald Reagan, for instance, who has so much in common with Dwight Eisenhower in terms of background and so on, was faced with completely different circumstances in 1980, when his mission was not to *restrain* the use of American power for long-range benefit in making friends but to *restore* American power. And so, he's less known for restraint and more in the spirit of TR [Teddy Roosevelt], sort of a swash-buckling free spirit in the Presidency. I think that Dwight Eisenhower had a conceptual grasp of history. I don't know where he got it, or how he learned it, or where he read it. He had a sense that America in 1953, was at a crossroads no country had ever been at, and that the circumstances required us to take the long-term view of this. We needed to think of our relations with friends twenty-five, thirty years from now, and to adopt the mode or the demeanor of restraint, rather than one of pounding our chests and saying "Look where we are."

R. Gordon Hoxie: Speaking of conceptual terms as David has so effectively done, let me give you one small example. That is when the Bricker Amendment was thrust upon President Eisenhower. In case you've forgotten, Bricker was a conservative Republican Senator from Ohio who wanted Presidents to no longer have the authority to enter into Executive agreements. Jim Hagerty was present and he told me this story. Eisenhower called in John Foster Dulles; they didn't know each other very well at that point: the Princeton-Brahmin and the man from Abilene. The President said, "How do you feel about this Bricker Amendment?" Well, Dulles was rather noncommittal, I guess he was feeling his way. Eisenhower said, "I'm going up to my quarters and do some reading tonight." "Up to my quarters," has some military overtones, but it happened to be the quarters of the White House. They met again the next day. Ike said, "Last night, I re-read from the Federalist Papers," and Dulles' glasses came down, startled at the President's scholarly research. Ike said, "Do you realize that if something like this Bricker Amendment goes through, that would put us back in the kind of a Presidency which existed under the Articles of Confederation, with an extremely weak executive?" Dulles just stammered, "Mr. President, you don't need a counsel, you are your own." Incidentally, that established a very interesting relationship. Although he put nothing in his memoirs of that meeting, there's a tiny footnote, maybe David has even overlooked it. All the footnote says is, "Early on, I discovered that John Foster Dulles must have started reading the Federalist Papers when he was in kindergarten." It became a sort of exchange between the two. I give that as an example of this person who could use history, who could use perception and use it most effectively.

Stephen Ambrose: Picking up on those comments and especially on something David said, one of the greatest strengths, perhaps *the* greatest, was his ability to take a long range view of things; this is virtually unique in American politics, where the politician's sense of the long range is who wins the next election. With Ike, it was a very much deeper look into the future. Some aspects of it, as you're all aware, are his sense of fiscal integrity and his old-fashioned horror of an unbalanced budget. That sense was based on his hopes for the future of the United States. In returning to my Victorian theme, he was a marvelous steward. You never caught Ike selling off the public lands. You never caught Ike opening up the national wilderness areas to exploitation. He, of course, was the creator of the soil bank, a marvelous program that I wish we had back. He said once that we must avoid plundering the resources of tomorrow for today's comfort. We want to pass on to our grandchildren an intact heritage. He followed that up with one of my very favorite of all his lines. He said, "We want democracy to survive for all ages to come." There just aren't very many politicians who would think, much less act, in those terms; and in that sense he was a very great builder; the Saint Lawrence Seaway, the Interstate Highway System and so much more.

Two other points off of this: First, Fred was quite right on that Gallup Poll of Ike's popularity and I think that it's important for scholars now that we're getting into post revisionism with Eisenhower, to understand this point. The American people never needed a revisionism of Ike. Liberal academics did. It was us, the young, hotshot professors, graduate students in the '50's, who needed to learn what a great man this was. The American people didn't need to learn that. They always had known it.

Now, one last negative about Ike and then Phillip wants to talk. On this negative, I think that the Democratic charge against Eisenhower that had the most force to it was, the eight years of the great postponement; the problems put off into the future. One of the best insights into Ike that I've ever had, I got from Andy Goodpaster who said that he once told Ike that "you know, Mr. President, problems put off for too long can become, when you finally turn to deal with them, unmanageable." I think that is true of civil rights and there are other areas in which that was the case in the 1950's.

Louis Galambos: Phil.

Phillip Henderson: I wanted to add a few footnotes to the discussion. Fred mentioned Eisenhower's advanced conceptual ability when it came to strategic questions. One of the memos I came across at the Eisenhower Library was from Eisenhower to the Acting Secretary of State in 1957 encouraging the Acting Secretary to read a new book by a young scholar named Henry Kissinger on nuclear weapons and foreign policy. He summarized the book in his memo in a very short way but it showed a grasp of the issues that Kissinger had raised in that book. As an addendum to what David was saying about his love of history, I think it should be noted that Eisenhower's peers in high school predicted that he would become a professor of history at Yale.

I also think we should mention Fox Connor's influence, General Fox Connor, who had given his own library in a sense to Eisenhower including von Clauswitz's *On War*, the *Federalist Papers*, and works by Rousseau and many other theorists.

David Eisenhower: Let me tell you something else that happened too along that line. There is a perspective in the man that's unusual and I think part of that has to do with the happenstance nature of his rise to prominence. It's an interesting biographical factor of Dwight Eisenhower that he spent fifty-three years of his life with conventional expectations, probably even diminished expectations, as his retirement approached in the army, and the war hadn't happened and this and that. He was from a family with a humble background. I'm saying that, by the age of 52 or 53 or so, your objectives are pretty set, your expectations are set. Then the next twenty-six years of his life, he led one of the great lives of the twentieth century. What I'm saying is he is not to the manor born. This is a fellow who, very late in life, suddenly encountered responsibilities that I just think he approached in a different spirit than someone coming along in his twenties or thirties, setting themselves on that course, and going out as a professional politician would do. I think on it as a certain aura of fatalism, I don't know how else to put it—a premonition about the few decisions that was his lot to make in life, all very important ones.

Louis Galambos: But he did a great deal (and that is one of the things that emerged from the research) to shape his own context and his own future.

David Eisenhower: And in a shorter period of time.

Louis Galambos: Yes.

David Eisenhower: And with many, many years spent in obscurity and preparation.

Stephen Ambrose: It is remarkable the patience the man had. A man of his ability, his ambition, his intelligence, his drive to be a major for fourteen years and to put up with it. Incidentally, here we return to the de Gaulle comparison. The same thing was true of de Gaulle. There is a wonderful story about Milton Eisenhower in the mid thirties, having a party in Washington. At the time, Milton was a bigshot. He was Number Two in the Department of Agriculture. In those years, Ike was known in Washington as

Milton's brother. Milton had a cocktail party and a reporter was about to leave. Milton grabbed him by the arm and said "don't leave yet, I want you to meet my brother. Why don't you keep your eye on him? He's going places." And the reporter shook hands with the then forty-seven-year-old Major and thought to himself "if he's going places, he'd better get started soon."

Fred Greenstein: When he went places, he went very rapidly which is another striking thing about him. There is, I agree, that long period of tutelage and it's critical to understand the fact that he spent a period with apparently a very impressive mentor, this fellow Fox Connor. Probably by negative example, he learned a great deal by being so close to Douglas MacArthur for so many years. At the point where he, himself, seemed to think that his career was about to end and that he might be ready to retire, World War II broke out; then, I think one can't understate the rapidity of his rise. He is called to Washington, almost on Pearl Harbor Day itself, by Marshall. Marshall says "give me your views, Eisenhower." By afternoon, Eisenhower has written a marvelously penetrating, extremely brief memo in which it states the conceptualization of World War II; mainly, Europe first, Asia secondary; but don't lose the Philippines because of the essence of public relations and the moral value of the Philippines; or rather, don't lose them without a fight, which was a very pressing image. Within six months, he is in England and he is up the vortex and dealing with the international figures in a position that is military in the technical sense but political in the highest sense of the word. I believe that it is one thing to say that Eisenhower is not a politician but by that we mean he is not a politician in some base, corrupt logrolling fashion. If politics is also, as Aristotle put it, the master science, and converges with what is commonly called statesmanship, those were his qualities. They were qualities of asking how you get things done in this world. A lot of his strength was the quality of balance, of weighing one thing against another, of not being an extremist, of thinking about long run-short run. *(Turning to David Eisenhower)* Now, when you started this, I thought you were actually hinting for something that would get us toward what might be some of the insights from Eisenhower for the present Gulf crisis and for other types of episodes.

Louis Galambos: I think we've done a good bit of that and we'll probably do more.

Fred Greenstein: There's something that I just mentioned there and that is we're all captured by Nixon in his book *Six Crises* where he said "this was a man whose mind could range over options in such a way that he seemed sometimes to be advancing hairbrained notions. But that was at the stage of thinking about what to do. When it came to deciding, he was as cautious and as shrewd and reasoned as anyone could be." I believe we see that sort of thing in the ending of the Korean War; in the Dien Bien Phu crisis, in the game of "bluff and chicken" and so on, of the offshore islands, in his conception of nuclear weapons. It would have been interesting if you could have continued such a mind through subsequent years.

R. Gordon Hoxie: May I say that there are five years, and I say that with all respect to the distinguished scholars here, but there are five years in his life which are virtually omitted in comment which I believe were years of great growth and this has been the view of some of the persons who knew him when he was the Army Chief of Staff, which he was immediately before he became the President of Columbia University. We forget that he was the President of Columbia University for five years and he was the President of Columbia University until the week before he came down to Washington. He resided at 60 Morningside Drive in New York City before he did at 1600 Pennsylvania Avenue in Washington, D.C. Those were years of growth, of humanity. One of the things that impressed me particularly is that, shortly before his first inaugural, he wrote a prayer stating "Our concern shall be for all the people, regardless of station, race or calling." That side of Eisenhower had not been revealed in the Eisenhower as Chief of Staff. When the students at Columbia and the professor of historiography asked him to speak, he lectured about two famous graduates of Columbia: Alexander Hamilton and John Jay, who wrote *The Federalist Papers*. The Columbia years were years of growth.

Finally, just let offer a few observations on Eisenhower and civil rights. I wish Herb Brownell were up here to do it. I think we should remember this. a) the first civil rights act since the Civil War reconstruction came from whom? It came from Eisenhower. b) regarding that civil rights act, who were the two Senators ironically, who did more to emasculate and try to block it? Their names, I'm sorry to say, were Kennedy and Johnson. And so far as you say, well, he never came to reject *Plessy v. Ferguson*, but according to my friend, Herb Brownell, after long discussions, he did indeed, and of course he did away with segregation in the armed forces, he did away with segregation in D.C. You can say, well, he was laying the groundwork and I agree, for the future. But don't dismiss his concern and don't dismiss the agonizing over Little Rock and his firmness there and don't dismiss the fact that the best judges in the Federal courts in the past five decades, according to the American Bar Association, were the Eisenhower appointments to the Federal Judiciary.

David Eisenhower: William Rogers thinks that the phrase "with all deliberate speed" was Dwight Eisenhower's. He thinks he remembers seeing it penned on a memo that went back to the Department of Justice during the litigation. "With all deliberate speed" was picked up, I believe, out of a Justice Department memo and written into the speech I heard on the Warren opinion. I might be wrong about that but, if it were true, it would express the kind of the balances again on this issue—deliberate speed. In other words, he was somebody who was the creative one.

Louis Galambos: Phil, could you comment on civil rights? Then I want to get back to Steve, because I know he's got more to say about that.

Phillip Henderson: Well, there's a young scholar here from the University of Montana who presented a paper yesterday, Michael Mayer, who I think has a more enlightened view. He has mined the archives of the Eisenhower Library very thoroughly and I think he's providing at least a contrast to Burk's view of Eisenhower's record on civil rights. I'm not as familiar with that sort of revisionism because I haven't read extensively on the civil rights record, but I think that it will begin to take hold. I do think that I would tend to agree with Gordon Hoxie and David Eisenhower that, for the time of the 1950's, passing the Civil Rights Bill was a major achievement.

Fred Greenstein: Eisenhower was not a racist. As he recognized in himself, much of his adult life had been spent in the south when he was stateside or with southerners or in contacts where the views we have about racial equality didn't exist and so it's somewhat anachronistic to look at that the way it was. True if you look at some of the documents out of the Augusta Golf Course, where he was with his friends and the way they could pick the caddies in their little year book, and so on, it is just outrageously stereotyped, if not racist, by present standards. He had a warm, personal relationship with his valet, Mony, but, while he was never in the vanguard, he also never seemed to pull back. One gets the sense that, as he got older, he did realize that this was an area where he could have done better.

Steve knows well about questions of segregation during World War II, etc.

Louis Galambos: Steve. The ball is in your court, I think.

Stephen Ambrose: Everything you say is right. The Battle of the Bulge. Ike was the one who said we're going to get these black troops into the front lines where they want to be. Beetle Smith went through the roof on this, there's no doubt about that. Ike appointed Earl Warren; and then there is that very famous quote of his that so many people use about "the biggest mistake I ever made was the appointment of that dumb son of a bitch, Earl Warren." He wasn't referring to *Brown v. Topeka* when he said that, he was referring to the Miranda case and other later decisions. His contribution is enormous just with the appointment of Earl Warren if nothing else. That he had the best Attorney General this country has ever had make the case before the Supreme Court in *Brown v. Topeka* is obviously very much to Ike's credit. As Gordon said, in 1957, he did guide through the first civil rights bill since reconstruction and it *was* weakened by Kennedy and Johnson. The Republicans were ready to go for a much tougher bill. I think perhaps most important of all, in 1957, at Little Rock, he let the segregationists know that they could not use force to maintain their system, that he was going to uphold the law. Now, having said all that, it remains true he was our leader. He wanted to be our leader. He fought for that nomination and he fought to win the election and he became our leader but, on this one issue, he abandoned leadership. He never stood before the American people and said that I think that segregation is morally wrong. I lived in the south in those years as a Yankee abolitionist. I went down to LSU to study with Harry

Williams in 1957, the critical year. If I heard it once, I heard it five thousand times from my fellow graduate students at LSU: the President himself doesn't believe in this.

Phillip Henderson: But I think that may relate more to Fred's observation that Eisenhower was reluctant to use the "bully pulpit" which...

Stephen Ambrose: And there comes a time when you've got to use it. And everybody in this audience, I dare say, who was in the south in those years will second what I've just said. That it made an enormous difference in the south that the President never spoke up.

Fred Greenstein: I think that's another place where you see even more exquisitely perhaps, the "bully pulpit" question. It was in his relations with McCarthy where, of course, he's most conventionally criticized. I don't think you can overstate the extent to which we now know specific things, that we didn't know at the time, which Eisenhower was doing or trying to do to combat McCarthy. If there ever was a point where "Hidden Hand" was very specifically in action and you can see it in detail, it is particularly during the period of the Army-McCarthy hearings. You can see it because Press Secretary Hagerty, who was Eisenhower's intermediary in such activities, just happened to keep a very detailed diary. There's also a little addition to your question about lying, or your observation about lying. There is at least a third case; and that is at one point in early 1954, the year that culminates from the McCarthy standpoint, McCarthy's censure by the Senate and his disappearance into political oblivion. In the spring of that year, Harry Truman at one point said, "McCarthy is the Republican Party's best asset." Well, the first thing Monday morning after that weekend statement of Truman's, Eisenhower is on the phone and he's calling the heads of CBS and NBC and saying McCarthy will be after you for air time. I want you not to give it to him but to give it to the Republican National Committee for a reply. Well, that led to a whole maneuver in which Eisenhower also coerced Richard Nixon to make a speech at that point. He didn't want to but he became the speaker responding to Truman but responding in a way which was an attack on McCarthy. It was somewhat offensively worded. It was that you've got to shoot rats but if you shoot them you have to know how to shoot straight. At any rate, it was an attack, it was by Nixon and it was planned, if not in that particular terminology, by Eisenhower and it was just a piece of the whole Hidden Hand thing. Now in the press conference, he was asked what he knew about this controversy in which McCarthy is saying, "they're denying me free air time." He says, "I don't have anything to do about the decisions the FCC makes." Well, this is just ingenuous, if not true.

Now, Eisenhower was not just prevailed upon but implored by people he had admired enormously, and most of all his brother, Milton, to speak out against McCarthy and he could not have been clearer in what he said. He said, if you attack such an individual, you provide them with exactly what they're looking for, namely, the visibility and attention and you dignify them. The way to deal with them is not to dignify them with a response. Now, I think that there was an important element to that. I believe that one reason that McCarthy got more and more unhinged was because he kept shooting at a target that was pretending that he didn't exist. His failure was not coming out and making statements about the evils of McCarthy-like phenomenon. Eisenhower made some of these late in the episode in a Columbia speech but he didn't speak in a way that would have, for instance, inspired the confidence of the Civil Service who were being so severely maligned. We know that morale in the Civil Service and Foreign Service was abysmal and that was well recognized in that period. So there was an up side/down side there.

Louis Galambos: David, what do you think about the McCarthy issue? I know you mentioned civil rights. Do you feel that that's one of those areas where there could have been more forceful action?

David Eisenhower: Well, I think McCarthy is part of the story. There are two dimensions of the Cold War. One is our relations with the external war, with the Soviet Union and the other is our resolution of that issue within our own bosom, within the United States, and McCarthy bore on that. I think the great difficulty here, the unspoken difficulty, as it seems to me, is that if there was going to be a break between McCarthy and Eisenhower, McCarthy had to initiate it. There was a theory, widespread and with some foundation, throughout 1952, that Dwight

Eisenhower was the leading edge of a Democratic conspiracy to seize control of the Republican party. I think there is something in this. He had served Roosevelt, he had been Truman's informal chairman of the JCS, he had held positions of great confidence and trust in the Democratic administration and now he's asking the Republican Party for their nomination and he is going to be *their* instrument to return to power. It seemed bizarre to the rank and file Republicans. Dwight Eisenhower was also probably the target of much of what McCarthy said. In the same way, the Morganthall planned controversies in late 1947 appeared to be aimed at warning Eisenhower away from trying to move into the Republican Party. McCarthy's antics in '51 and '52 were aimed at deterring an Eisenhower bid in 1952 as well. The antagonism between the two men was revealed in the papers and is beyond dispute. The question is, who takes the initiative and for what reason? A good comparison would be between Eisenhower and George Marshall after their tiff and very painful breakdown. Marshall would rather be right than president. He was a Nobel Prize winner, was he not? He won the Nobel Peace Prize in 1953 and he was that kind of man who would have denounced McCarthy had he been given a political forum. Eisenhower is the compromiser, he *is* the politician and he's an effective President for eight years. That's the trade off. Dwight Eisenhower could not govern the nation between 1953 and 1957, repudiated by half of the Republican Party any more than Lyndon Johnson could govern the nation in 1968 repudiated by half of his party. As I see it, it's a question of initiative. The way to avoid it was to allow McCarthy to finally say "you don't represent us," and then test the issue. Then, after it was over, there was pressure on granddad to make a great moral at McCarthy's expense. My question is: who would it have made look good and who would it have made look bad? I think that moral this and that can be deployed very selectively. I think Steve Ambrose had a good point in civil rights, where it can have an impact on people and actually move people toward resolving an issue or making progress. On the McCarthy issue, making a moral at McCarthy's expense at practically any point in '54, might have made Eisenhower look better long range, but he was deterred from that. The Hagerty diary I think even shows that Hagerty restrained Eisenhower in May and June of 1954, from lashing out at McCarthy because "it doesn't matter now and all this can do is really make you look bad long range and attempt to look good short range." So I think it was up to McCarthy.

R. Gordon Hoxie: Just one note from his brother, Milton Eisenhower, a great educator and president of three major universities. Milton said to me on more than one occasion, "yes, Ike and I saw eye to eye on almost everything. The only real difference between us was (and this may surprise some) he was more liberal in his outlooks than I was." I believe there is much in that statement. Finally, I realize we're running out of time, I would just like to say since so many people from the academic world who are studying Eisenhower and who are here from throughout the nation that I think James David Barber made a great, great error in 1969, when he pegged Ike as being a passive/negative. Fortunately, others countered it; people who have found that the simple truth of the matter is that he was the most activist, politically, of the modern presidents with the possible exception of FDR; and, perhaps *with* the possible exception of FDR, the most skilled politically of the modern presidents. I'm absolutely convinced of that fact. He is *exactly* the opposite of what Barber conveyed him and I think we still have to overcome on that score; but he was an extremely skilled person politically. Looking back on it, George Reedy, Johnson's assistant as a Minority Leader and as a Majority Leader and his press secretary, said that Eisenhower was absolutely masterful in his political skills.

Louis Galambos: Steve.

Stephen Ambrose: I would like very much to second that and I agree entirely about Barber. There is no question whatsoever in my mind that Dwight Eisenhower was the best president of the second half of the twentieth century. He was an activist president and he was a building president and we're still operating off of the infrastructure that he has built and it has been absolutely all downhill ever since 1961. Now, having said that, let's go back to Joe McCarthy for a second. Ike said at an academy once in '53 that there comes a time when you've just got to speak up. Unfortunately, he never did it with regard to McCarthy; speak up in public, that is. We all know about Fred's work, and what he has shown and the way he has worked through the "day by day" on what Ike did to undercut McCarthy; and that's all true. But now, getting back to the bully pulpit: it hurts; and there are people in this audience, I know, who felt it at the time: it hurts. The malarkey, the excision of the paragraph praising George Marshall, because Joe McCarthy demanded that it be taken out. That hurts. And it hurts that Ike sat there during the Army-McCarthy hearings, while McCarthy said to General Zwicker, who had been on the beaches of Omaha, "You are not fit to wear the uniform of the United States Army" and Ike never said "boo" about it. And I fault him on that one.

Fred Greenstein: The purpose of this conference is to discuss Eisenhower's legacy. If he were asked what his legacy were, I'm quite sure it would be in national security and international relations which was certainly his primary preoccupation; this was very much a foreign relations presidency. One reason activism is a term which has been hard to apply to Eisenhower is because much of his activity was in the direction of preventing things. The major accomplishment, in his view, clearly was eight years without war and, I think he made it even more specific, without an American soldier being lost in combat. Now how that fits together with the fact that the Korean War had to be ended, I don't know; so I may not be faithfully capturing his terminology. Attention to matters of war and peace was always primary and Phil Henderson has done a nice job of bringing out the organizational element. Eisenhower would never have claimed that machinery, now by machinery I mean the foreign policy decision-making process, which was much more articulated and much more sophisticated in its organization than it had been before and than it has been since, he would never claim that that was what made for his success. What he said was "always rely on planning and never rely on plans." What he meant was that any event will take a unique quality. It has to be decided not by a committee, but by an individual. His great strength was in making those decisions. The greatest one he ever made was undoubtedly the D-Day decision and not any one that he made within his presidency; but you see that dynamic again and again.

Now to the question of where the organization and where the mustering of aides and so on fit together; and where I think there's an extremely important moral. It really makes me extremely uneasy as I look at the Bush presidency now as we face the Gulf episode. What seems to be lacking in the Bush presidency is the sense that the decision-making process of a few individuals, the President, the chairman of the JCS, the Secretary of State, the Secretary of Defense, and the Special Assistant, is not much in the sense that those guys are in a deeper structure. No matter how many people George Bush phones and networks, if he's not getting the best possible information from his own specialists, and information that's constantly flowing in, then there are major dangers and I'm thinking not so much at the moment about what has happened since the intervention but the whole question of whether Saddam Hussein could have been deterred. Now, we will never know but we do know that there were even major debates going on within the administration. In the Eisenhower process, those debates would have come up in the NSC meeting. They would have met every week and they would have been hammering tongs at it.

Phillip Henderson: It's striking the lack of rigor in the post Eisenhower period. Eisenhower argued that organization was a bulwark against chaos, confusion and failure. In the post Eisenhower period, starting with Lyndon Johnson's Tuesday luncheon meetings and Jimmy Carter's Vance, Brzezinksi and Brown breakfast meetings, policy has been made in such an informal way that clear records have not even been kept of decisions. I would add that there have been three major fiascos from the lack of a structured policy-making apparatus, and those would be the Bay of Pigs fiasco, the Carter Iran rescue attempt and the Iran arms sales under the Reagan administration.

Louis Galambos: Lest we be *too* negative about the recent past, I remind the panel that the Cold War seems to have ended and seems to have ended in our favor in certain regards and I wanted David to comment on what Ike would say if he could see recent developments in the Cold War.

David Eisenhower: Steve Ambrose has written extensively about World War II in his career and so have I and I'm sort of following in his footsteps in that respect. It's hard to experience World War II through the lens of the Eisenhower papers and the surrounding environment that one tries to re-create and think that Germany, German unification, is conceivable. On the one hand, I think that Dwight Eisenhower, just speculating or whatever, would have been surprised. On the other hand, I think that, at the root of the allied judgment of World War II, it was safe to make common cause with the Soviet Union against Germany. It was the idea that the Soviet Union, long range, would not prove to be the mortal enemy that Nazi Germany was and, given time, the Soviet Union would act rationally and that, if certain maneuvers involved the risk of the quote loss close quote of certain territories to the Soviet Union, in time, the Soviet Union would not attempt to maintain an artificial empire in that area. That was the basis of Roosevelt's decision to make common cause with the Soviet Union against the Germans and so, in a sense, the whole wisdom of that World War II policy has been vindicated now—fifty years later. One has to give Roosevelt or Churchill or Eisenhower or whoever, credit for at least sensing the implications of the course they were on.

Stephen Ambrose: Don't leave Harry Truman out.

David Eisenhower: Harry Truman. Well, he wasn't involved in war decisions. So, perhaps they would have expected it. I think Churchill would have. At the Tehran Conference, the most important conference of the war, I think, Stalin was pressing Churchill for a guarantee that Germany would never be able to rise and threaten world peace a third time and Churchill's reply was "no guarantee is possible because nothing is final. The world rolls on and all we can do is keep it safe for fifty years."

Fred Greenstein: On the matter of the end of the Cold War, certainly Dulles would not have been surprised given the reverse similar way that Kennett Dulles repeatedly was saying if we can deter and hold the line long enough that the system will fall of its weight, of its internal contradictions. Now, that is highly prescient and I don't remember a lot of statements of Eisenhower's although, I'm sure there were. Of course, the two of them became so close and their ideas were so intermingled that it would be impossible to believe that he didn't...

Stephen Ambrose: Let's not single out individuals. It's that whole generation of men that decided on the doctrine of containment and that was the whole idea of containment. They all collapsed eventually for the reason Ike said, that they're going to have to educate their people to stay up with the modern world and when they do that they're going to sow the seeds of their own destruction which has happened.

I want to go back very quickly to the point that Phil was making about organization and to make a little compare and contrast between Nixon and Eisenhower. Eisenhower brought everybody in as we have been emphasizing and heard all points of view before deciding. It is *remarkable* to go through Nixon's papers and see that he dealt with Bob Haldeman and John Ehrlichman and Henry Kissinger and Chuck Colson and that was just about it. He did not bring in that kind of consultation that Fred and Phil have been talking about, that Ike did, and I think that Nixon paid the price for that.

David Eisenhower: Nixon was a war time president and Eisenhower wasn't and that's the decisive difference between the two. The Nixon administration was organized for the purpose of resolving the Viet Nam War on an acceptable basis for the American people. Nixon had a complete free hand of pursuit of diplomacy and that's what it was. It wasn't a free hand of pursuit of military option or free hand to regiment the United States, it was to find a diplomatic exit from the Viet Nam War and so, he had a very closed administration. Eisenhower presided over the peace and prosperity of 1953 to 1961, so, of course, it was a different White House.

Louis Galambos: I think you can see, there are many historical questions left floating around and that we can't resolve all of these but I think that the panelists have done a super job and now I want to give the people out here a chance to ask them some questions and I think we have a procedure for doing that.

Shirley Anne Warshaw: If anyone has a question, would you please come up to the microphone and state your name before you ask your question.

Tom Wolfe: Good morning. I'm Tom Wolfe, the trustee of the Eisenhower Society, a co-sponsor of the events of this week. I have listened carefully to General Brownell and you gentlemen speak about the civil rights activism of Dwight Eisenhower and, personally, as an admirer and, in '52 a worker for Eisenhower, I liked General Brownell's description slightly better than some of the others I've heard. But assuming, which I can, that Dr. Ambrose is quite correct about the effect on the south and what

Eisenhower might have done, my question is: if he had been more activist and vocal about civil rights, would that have blunted his effectiveness in other pressing policies that he needed to support for those people that he would have antagonized with that activism.

Stephen Ambrose: That inquiry is right on the mark and he did have to govern with the help of the southern Democrats. This gets you into the whole problem that we're so concerned with today with the effect of divided government. That's absolutely right and I agree entirely. I can see Ike's point of view and I still wish that he had stood up and said that it's morally wrong to segregate the races. That's my politics.

R. Gordon Hoxie: In addition to the southern Democrats, he needed the support of the conservative wing of his own party and that was not the wing that he was comfortable in. He was in this liberal wing as were Dewey and Nelson Rockefeller and, of course as we know, the conservative wing in '64 did indeed capture policy control of the Republican party, which Eisenhower regretted.

Louis Galambos: We're back to your point, David, that if you see international relations as your main thrust and the main goal of your administration, you'll make a different calculation about domestic policies.

David Eisenhower: I think, probably in his own mind he's thinking, "my record on civil rights—the test is, does it make this issue easier or more difficult for my successor" and I think that the action in Little Rock is the key here. By indicating that federal troops were available to enforce integration of schools, I think he made it much easier for the Kennedy administration to desegregate graduate schools and to begin the implementation of *Brown*. What he did was done reluctantly and he was not confident about his ability to act in this area that wasn't in his expertise or interest but he moved methodically to prepare the issue for the civil rights president. Kennedy was not someone who was notably eloquent on this issue, or he's been criticized for being reticent on the question of civil rights. I would argue that Kennedy, by virtue of his election in 1960, represented tremendous progress in civil rights. He was the youngest elected president, he was Irish Catholic, one taboo after another fell as

John Kennedy took office and his survival in office, popularity and so on, was very much a key aspect of the civil rights progress in this country. In the same way, Dwight Eisenhower, elected in 1952, with all the anomalies that he had in facing Senator McCarthy, his survival in office for 4 or 6 years represented progress there and I'm suggesting that parallel between the two.

Betty Glad: I'm Betty Glad from the University of South Carolina and I work on other presidencies and am just new at looking at Eisenhower. I'm very much impressed with his intelligence, skills and with Fred Greenstein's description of his tactics of the Hidden Hand presidency. But I wonder if there are not some general limits to the tactics of using the Hidden Hand aside from the issues you have discussed; for example, Chip Bohlen at one time had a meeting with Eisenhower. He told Dulles that Tom Visajenning wanted to talk to him about Scott McLeod in the State Department. When he saw Eisenhower, he said "I have one issue here." Ike immediately knew he wanted to talk about Scott McLeod, and he said "well, it was probably a mistake in appointing him in the first place but it would create such a stink to get rid of him now that I can't do it." I also think that perhaps he had some problems with Allen Dulles of his Foreign Intelligence Advisory Board in late 1956, and said Dulles was not a good administrator. You should split the job, have Dulles in charge of covert operations and somebody else to be the manager and coordinator of intelligence but Eisenhower didn't want to move on that particular issue. So, I'm wondering if sometimes his concern for not creating political problems in a sense led to other deficiencies in the administration that he would have handled better had he moved on them.

Louis Galambos: Phillip. You get the final word on this.

Phillip Henderson: I would defer to Fred on this question.

Louis Galambos: Fred. He's deferred to you.

Fred Greenstein: I just assumed it was a question to me because of the various personal references. What you describe, Betty, is not so much hidden hand maneuvers themselves as the general mentality behind them which is not to make ripples. I believe that was powerfully ingrained in him at the cost of his need in his earlier years as a military leader, to have a political impact but not to present it as a political impact. There is a great microcosm in the papers that Galambos edited of the McCarthy episode and an episode in which Mark Clark was up for one more star before Congress but was under attack by the virulent racist Mississippi Congressman, John Rankin, for his role in something called the Rapido River Crossing and Clark wanted to reply to this assault to his character and Eisenhower says "please don't say anything. I believe I've worked this out behind the scenes. I've talked to the boys and it will go through but if you respond to Rankin it will all blow up and, if it's necessary, I will go up to the Hill to testify for you. I think I will speak about infantry tactics at Pickett's Charge." He was going to Stonewall them by talking about the Battle of Gettysburg, even if he did go up. But at some point, I think that mode becomes too cautious. It's very hard to judge his specific instances and those may be perfect examples of where it would have worked better to be up front.

Louis Galambos: I think that's an excellent point in Gettysburg for us to conclude. We've reached the end of our time. These brilliant scholars will stay and answer all of your questions and I think we ought to thank them for a terrific discussion.

Biographies

Martin Agronsky is a highly respected newsman and documentary producer who has been involved in television since the early 1950's. From 1952-1969, he was a Foreign Correspondent for NBC, a Washington Correspondent for ABC, and Documentary Producer for CBS. He has also served as the host of his own program on PBS, "Agronsky and Company."

Stephen E. Ambrose has written several of the foremost books and articles about President Eisenhower and has spoken at universities throughout the United States and Europe. He has also served as the author and consultant of several TV documentaries on World War II and the Cold War. He is a member of several boards and historical associations. He is currently a professor of history and Director of the Eisenhower Center at the University of New Orleans.

Ralph C. Bledsoe was a Special Assistant to President Reagan and Executive Secretary of the Domestic Policy Council between 1985 and 1988. From 1982 to 1985, he was Assistant Director for Management and Administration at the White House office of Policy Development, Executive Secretary of the Cabinet Council on Management and Administration, and Executive Director of the Federal Property Review Board. He was Associate Director of the White House Office of Planning and Evaluation from 1981 to 1982. He is currently Director of the Eisenhower Library in Simi Valley, California.

Herbert Brownell was Attorney General of the United States under President Eisenhower from 1953-1957. He was campaign manager for Governor Dewey in the 1944 and 1948 presidential elections and was involved with the Eisenhower Campaign in 1952. He has served the nation as a member of such commissions as the Second Hoover Commission on Reorganization of the Executive Branch of the Federal Government.

He was the principal author of the 25th Amendment to the U.S. Constitution relating to presidential disability.

Robert F. Burk is an associate professor of history at Muskingum College in New Concord, Ohio. He is the author of several books and articles concerning the Eisenhower Presidency.

James M. Cannon was Assistant to President Ford for Domestic Affairs and Executive Director at the Domestic Council from 1975 to 1977. He was Chief of Staff for U.S. Senate Majority Leader Howard H. Baker, Jr., advising the Senator on policy and political issues. In 1988, he served as Executive Director of the American Agenda, a bipartisan policy committee to assist the President-elect. Most recently, he served as the Director of the Eisenhower Centennial Foundation.

Charles W. Corddry is the dean of American Defense correspondents. He first covered defense and foreign affairs in Washington for United Press and has done so for the *Baltimore Sun* since 1967. He has been a panelist on the award-winning "Washington Week in Review," public television's longest-running program. He continues to speak out on political-military issues at educational institutions and conferences. In 1988, he received the Gerald R. Ford Foundation Prize for Distinguished Reporting on National Defense—Lifetime Achievement.

Robert J. Donovan was White House correspondent and then Washington Bureau Chief for both the *New York Herald Tribune* and the *Los Angeles Times*. He has been a Fellow at the Woodrow Wilson School of Public and International Affairs and of the Woodrow Wilson International Center for Scholars. The author of several books on American political life, he has been a Ferris Professor of Journalism at Princeton University.

D. David Eisenhower is the grandson of President Dwight D. Eisenhower and a son-in-law of President Richard Nixon. He is a graduate of Amherst College and the George Washington University School of Law. Between 1970 and 1973, he served in the Navy as an officer aboard the U.S.S. Albany and is currently working on a three-volume history of the Eisenhower years of which *Eisenhower: At War 1943-1945* is the first.

William Bragg Ewald, Jr. served as Special Assistant on the White House Staff and as assistant to President Eisenhower in the preparation of his memoirs. He served as Assistant to the Secretary of the Interior. His awards include the Eisenhower Exchange Fellowship for the Study of the United States Government's educational, informational, and cultural programs in several countries. He has also served in senior management positions for IBM.

Arthur Flemming served as Director of the Office of Defense Mobilization from 1953-1957 and as Secretary of Health, Education and Welfare from 1958-1961. He remained active in civil rights after leaving the White House, serving as Chairman of the U.S. Commission on Civil Rights from 1974 to 1981. In addition, Dr. Flemming has served as President of Ohio Wesleyan University, President of the University of Oregon and President of Macalester College.

Louis Galambos, an esteemed historian from the Johns Hopkins University, is the editor of *The Papers of Dwight David Eisenhower*. He served as a Woodrow Wilson Center Fellow from 1985-1986 and is the author of several books and articles on economic history.

Fred I. Greenstein is the author of the heralded book *The Hidden-Hand Presidency: Eisenhower as Leader*. He is currently a Professor of Politics at Princeton University and is the author of several books and articles on the Presidency.

Thomas C. Griscom served as President Reagan's Assistant for Communications from 1987-1988. He has also held the positions of Press Secretary to U.S. Senator Howard Baker, President and Chief Operating Officer of Ogilvy and Mather Public Affairs, and Executive Director of the National Republican Senatorial Campaign Committee.

Phillip G. Henderson is the author of many books and articles concerning the Presidency, including *Managing the Presidency: The Eisenhower Legacy—From Kennedy to Reagan.* He has served as a panelist and discussant at several conferences and symposia dealing with the Presidency.

Stephen Hess has served the United States Government in numerous ways, most recently as a Senior Fellow at The Brookings Institution. He has served as a U.S. Representative in the UN General Assembly, and as Staff Assistant to the President (number-two speech writer) from 1959-1961. He has served as a participant on several U.S. cultural missions. He is the author of books and articles concerning the Presidency and other aspects of the Federal government.

R. Gordon Hoxie was the founder and has served since 1969 as President and Chief Executive Officer of the Center for the Study of the Presidency. He was also the founder of *Presidential Studies Quarterly* and has served as its Editor since its inception in 1971. Earlier, he had served as President of C. W. Post College, which he also helped found. He has served as a consultant to both the Department of State and the Department of Defense. He is the author, editor and contributor to publications on the American Presidency.

David C. Kozak is currently Director of the Institute for Policy and Leadership Studies at Gannon University in Erie, Pennsylvania. He is author, editor and contributor to numerous books, articles and essays on American politics. He was a 1981-1982 Congressional Fellow, serving on the staffs of Congressmen Jim Lloyd (D., Calif.) and Andy Jacobs (D., Ind.) and Senator James Exon (D., Neb.). He served as policy analyst to the Secretary of the Air Force (1986), as co-director of the Taft Institute for Teachers at Gannon University (1988, 1989), and as consultant, National Public Affairs, the Chautauqua Institution (1988 to present). He serves on the National Advisory Board and as program consultant for the Center for the Study of the Presidency.

Bradley H. Patterson, Jr. served as Assistant Cabinet Secretary at the White House from 1954 to 1961. In the fall of 1969, he rejoined the White House staff and was closely involved with civil rights and Indian affairs. He was later appointed Assistant Director of the White House Office of Presidential Personnel. He is a member of the American Political Science Association and of the Center for the Study of the Presidency.

Maxwell M. Rabb served as Ambassador to Italy from 1981 to 1989. He served President Eisenhower as Secretary of the Cabinet in the White House from 1953-1958. Since then, he has served in every national administration. Ambassador Rabb has received numerous awards and commendations for his achievements.

Andy Rooney has been described by *Time* magazine as "the most felicitous non-fiction writer in television." He has been with CBS since 1959 and has received much acclaim for his unique reports, "A Few Minutes With Andy Rooney." In addition to his work in television, he has been active in radio, books, magazine articles, and war correspondence. He covered Europe for *Stars and Stripes* while General Eisenhower was serving as Commander of the Armed Forces.

Raymond J. Saulnier served as Chairman of President Eisenhower's Council of Economic Advisors from 1956-1961. Before holding that position, he served as Director of the Financial Research Program for the National Bureau of Economic Research from 1946-1953. He has also served on Presidential Commissions and task forces.

Ray Scherer was NBC White House Correspondent during the Eisenhower Administration. He was the only television correspondent on the scene in Denver when President Eisenhower had his 1955 heart attack and covered all of the President's global journeys in 1959 and 1960. He began covering Presidents for NBC during the Truman years and continued until 1969.

Daniel Schorr's journalistic accomplishments are numerous. Throughout his career, which has spanned a half century, he has covered events ranging from the McCarthy hearings and the Iran-Contra affair to superpower summits between Eisenhower and Khrushchev and Reagan and Gorbachev. In 1955, he received accreditation to open a CBS bureau in Moscow, climaxing with a first-ever exclusive television interview with Soviet leader Nikita Khrushchev. In 1960, he was assigned as CBS bureau chief in Bonn, Germany and Eastern Europe and covered the building of the Berlin Wall. In 1979, he helped create the Cable News Network, serving in Washington as its senior correspondent until 1985. He is currently senior news analyst for National Public Radio.

Glenn T. Seaborg won the 1951 Nobel Prize in Chemistry for his work on the chemistry of transuranium elements. Dr. Seaborg served as the Chairman of the Atomic Energy Commission under Presidents Kennedy, Johnson and Nixon. He is the author of several noteworthy books and numerous articles and is currently Professor of Chemistry (the most distinguished title bestowed by the Regents) at the University of California, Berkeley.

Rocco C. Siciliano served as an Assistant Secretary of Labor under the Eisenhower Administration from 1953 through 1957. In 1957, he moved to the White House as Special Assistant to the President for Personnel Management. Mr. Siciliano also served as Under Secretary of the U.S. Department of Commerce under President Nixon from Jan. 1965 to March 1971. He now serves as a member of the Board of Directors of the Eisenhower World Affairs Institute and as a Trustee of the National Academy of Public Administration.

Elmer B. Staats served as Executive Officer of the National Operations Security Council under President Eisenhower from 1953-1958. He has served the Bureau of the Budget in several capacities, including Assistant Director and Deputy Director. From 1966-1981, he held the position of Comptroller

General of the United States. He is currently active on many boards of directors throughout the country.

Robert C. Wood served as Secretary of Housing and Urban Development from 1968-1969. He has had a successful career in academia, serving as a school system superintendent and university president. He has also been the Chairman of a major transportation authority. He has written numerous works on political and urban issues.

INDEX